UNDERSTANDING ACCOUNTING ETHICS

A New Approach to

UNDERSTANDING

ACCOUNTING ETHICS

Principles-based accounting

Professionalism

Pride

by

MARK CHEFFERS, C.P.A., A.B.V.

MICHAEL PAKALUK, Ph.D. (Philosophy)

ALLEN DAVID PRESS ~ MANCHAUG, MASSACHUSETTS
2005

Published in the United States by
Allen David Press
9 Main Street
Manchaug, MA 01526

ISBN 0-9765280-0-2

Printed in the United States of America

To

Allen and Ruth

- *Why isn't it enough if I simply follow the rules?*

- *What makes an accountant a professional?*

- *If it's a judgment call, is it subjective?*

- *What do we mean by the 'public interest'?*

- *Why is good character crucially important?*

- *What constitutes a practitioner's 'integrity'?*

- *Why is independence essential?*

- *But can ethics be taught?*

Contents

Executive Summary

THIS BOOK IS A STUDY OF ETHICS for the accounting profession, with attention both to law and personal choice. Using the notion of a 'virtue', it explains how the code of ethics for accountants follows from the distinctive role that accountants play in society. It illustrates these ideas through case studies, especially of Enron and WorldCom. It offers definite proposals for teaching ethics to accounting professionals.

What follows here is an executive summary of each chapter, including representative quotations from each chapter. Readers are encouraged to read at first those chapters that most interest them and then later attend to the argument of the book as a whole.

Chapter 1: Introduction

Recent accounting scandals have precipitated reforms in the accounting profession, some involving oversight agencies and laws that operate 'from the outside', others that involve attention to principles and ideals 'from the inside.' The latter must include a return to principles-based accounting; a renewed sense of professionalism; and an appropriate pride in the profession. All of these in turn require attention to the ethical foundations of accounting.

~ "Professionalism is fundamentally an ethical orientation, implying integrity and adherence to high ideals. Thus, any reform that attempts to articulate, once again, the highest ideals of professionalism for an accountant, must necessarily pay careful attention to ethics. There can be no true professionalism without attention to ethics." *(pp. 16-17)*

~ "An accountant's 'philosophy' is important for achieving unity of life. One needs to consider: Is accountancy a profession that can serve as the organizing principle of a worthwhile human life?" *(p. 22)*

Chapter 2: From Rules to Principles

It's not enough that a practitioner simply 'follow the rules', no matter how detailed or subtle those rules may be. Rules are necessary for correct action, but not sufficient. The key question to consider is: Are rules in the service of principles, or do rules trump principles? Clearly, rules have to be in the service of principles. But it follows from this a practitioner must continually rely on the sort of good judgment that involves an appropriate ethical commitment.

~ "It is clear, then, that it would not be possible for someone to act with intelligence and integrity, by simply trying to follow rules, no matter how well crafted or carefully qualified those rules may be. Someone who is attempting to follow rules must, at nearly every point, rely on good judgment, draw upon deeper principles, and view his action in relation to various idealizations. The ability to do this well is an ethical capacity. Thus, simply to follow rules well requires an appropriate ethical orientation." *(p. 32)*

~ "The interpretation of any rule requires an appeal to how a reasonable person would judge or view things." *(p. 36)*

~ "A fairly clear example of the importance of good character generally for a practitioner has to do with greed. We may define greed as the desire or wish to have 'as much wealth as possible'. Greed therefore is of its nature unlimited; it is never truly satisfied. Greed is not, for instance, a desire for the exact capital needed for

2

some specific enterprise; neither is it a desire for a sufficiency of wealth to raise a family with moderate advantages and ease. Both of these desires are limited, and when one reaches the stipulated amount, the desire vanishes. But greed, as is well recognized, is never satisfied. It sets goals for itself, but once these are met, it immediately is dissatisfied and looks for more." *(p. 44)*

Chapter 3: Elements of Ethics

Accounting ethics is a branch of ethics in general, so some fundamentals of ethics must first be considered. A 'virtue based' approach to ethics is best suited to the study of accounting ethics, rather than the chief alternatives, utilitarianism or Kantianism. A virtue may be defined as a trait which enables something (or someone) to carry out its distinctive task well. Something that has the requisite virtues is a good thing of that kind. But the virtue of a thing needs to be considered in relation to the 'common good' and to the law which governs the associations of which it is a part.

~ "Typically, we acquire a virtue of character by doing the relevant sorts of actions in some restricted or less significant field of action. A child, for instance, develops honesty by being truthful about relatively small and insignificant matters. A recruit grows in courage by field exercises which are successively closer in character to actual battle conditions. Because typically we acquire traits of character in relatively minor situations, indirectly related to those circumstances in which it is most important to exercise those traits, it happens that scrupulously good behavior in minor details ends up being very important for the development and maintenance of virtues of character." *(p. 73)*

~ "People form an association in order to procure some good, or enjoy a service, or achieve a result, that each could not attain at all, or attain easily, on his own." *(p. 75)*

~ "Every association involves reciprocity. Each member gives up trying to achieve some good on his own; he consents to receive it through the association; and therefore he directs his efforts at some coordinated plan of action required by the association." *(p. 75)*

Chapter 4: Basics of Accounting Ethics

The virtues of an accountant, then, are those traits that enable a practitioner to carry out well the distinctive task of accountancy. But what is that task? It is the fostering of trust that is necessary for the sound operation of commerce and the marketplace. This trust is an 'honorable' good, not an instrumental good. As a result, accounting is a profession and not a business. That an accountant needs to be objective, independent, and have integrity, follows from these considerations. The virtues of an accountant include both 'intellectual' traits, and traits of character.

~ "'Obviously no one can claim to be a member of a profession, or expect to succeed in one, unless he is prepared, when necessary, to subordinate his own interest to that of his client.... The high-minded accountant who undertakes to practice in this field assumes high ethical obligations, and it is the assumption of such obligations that makes what might otherwise be a business, a profession. Of all the group of professions which are closely allied with business, there is none in which the practitioner is under a greater ethical obligation to persons who are not his immediate clients; and it is for this reason I believe accounting ought, and can be made, to take an outstanding position in this group.'—George Oliver May (in 'The Accountant and the Investor', 1932)" *(p. 87)*

~ "But there are some goods that have a value that cannot be measured in terms of instrumental goods. Health is obviously of that sort: good health is not on the same level as instrumental goods, because good health is a precondition for enjoying any instrumental good at all. Other goods that are incommensurable with instrumental goods are such things as knowledge; human rights; freedom; justice; religious worship. Call these 'honorable' goods (from the Latin, *bonum honestum*). It is a mark of a profession that it aims at a good of that sort, which is incommensurably higher than instrumental goods." *(p. 89)*

~ "Accounting is a profession because it aims at knowledge, insofar as it verifies that some presentation of the position of a company is accurate and representative; and because the trust which accounting makes possible is a precondition of the good operation of the

4

marketplace (call this the 'public trust'). Knowledge and trust are not instrumental goods; therefore, accounting is a profession." *(p. 89)*

~ "The payment that a professional receives for services has more of the character of an honorarium or stipend than a strict equivalent. Strictly, the work of a professional cannot be compensated for by money, because money is only an instrumental good, but a professional provides an incommensurably higher good." *(p. 90)*

~ "By certifying the public reports that collectively depict a corporation's financial status, the independent auditor assumes a public responsibility transcending any employment relationship with the client. The independent public accountant performing this special function owes ultimate allegiance to the corporation's creditors and stockholders, as well as to the investing public. This 'public watchdog' function demands that the accountant maintain total independence from the client at all times and requires complete fidelity to the public trust." *(U.S. v. Arthur Young)* *(p. 104)*

Chapter 5: Enron, a Failure of Objectivity and Independence

A practitioner must be concerned not simply with independence in fact, but also with the appearance of independence. The reason is that when a practitioner's independence seems to be compromised, then that practitioner is precisely not well positioned to judge whether it really is so. Enron's rapid collapse, and the corresponding demise of Andersen, teach these truths all too well.

~ "Watkins is an employee of Enron, but as a professional CPA, she has a responsibility to the Public Interest that transcends her employment there. It is not clear, however, that her concerns for her own standing ever rise to the level of professional integrity; they seem to be phrased more in terms of her career: 'My 8 years of Enron work history will be worth nothing on my resume,' she writes to Lay, 'the business world will consider the past successes as nothing but an elaborate accounting hoax.'" *(p. 122)*

~ "The relevant accounting rule at the time stipulated that SPEs, to be truly independent, had to have at least 3% outside equity. But this is a necessary condition, not a sufficient condition of independence.   *If an entity cannot be regarded as independent if it fails to have 3% equity, it does not follow that it will always be independent if it does have 3% equity.*   The rule must be treated as a good starting point, which guides but does not substitute for professional judgment." *(p. 123)*

~ "[T]he argument that an accountant's liability in law should be more restricted than the extent of public reliance upon an accountant's work, can ultimately make sense only if there exist strong and demonstrably effective safeguards already in place, internal to the profession of accounting itself, so that legal protection of the investor's reasonable expectation becomes unnecessary." *(p. 128)*

Chapter 6: WorldCom, a Failure of Professionalism and Integrity

Professionalism and integrity imply a commitment to the public interest that transcends the demands of one's employer or client.   The WorldCom fraud involved none of the accounting pyrotechnics which marked Enron SPEs, but it did require a dramatic lapse from professionalism on the part of many CPAs within WorldCom, and a lack of due diligence on the part of its external auditor.

~ "[T]he WorldCom scandal was made possible because some accountants failed to live the virtues of accountancy, and failed to adhere to the principles and ideals of their profession. Worse than this: Ebbers, Sullivan, and Myers presumed that it would be so. Even in a post-Enron environment, they acted on the presumption that the accountants whose cooperation they needed to perpetrate their fraud would not oppose them (at the price of losing their jobs), or would turn a blind eye, or would even assist them—and, sad to say, they were proved right in this." *(p. 148)*

Chapter 7: Can Accounting Ethics Be Taught?

If ethics in accounting involves acquiring both 'intellectual' virtues and the virtues of character, then ethics can be taught if these things can be taught. But they can indeed be taught. Intellectual virtues can be taught through good instruction, attention to case studies, and apprenticeship to senior practitioners who display good judgment. Virtues of character can be acquired by scrupulous attention to upright choices in small matters and in 'first steps'. Ethics can in this way be integrated into the complete education and professional development of a practitioner.

~ "But the question of whether accounting ethics in particular can be taught hinges on what we mean by accounting ethics. As Plato pointed out similarly in the *Meno*, the question of whether virtue can be taught depends upon our answer to the question, 'What is virtue?'" *(p. 166)*

~ "[E]thical accounting involves understanding; idealism; character; and culture. So the question of whether accounting ethics can be taught resolves into the question of whether any or all of these components can be 'taught' and, if so, how they can be 'taught'. But it is clear that they can be taught." *(p. 167)*

~ "Character ... is formed by and tested in small things and first things. This component of ethical accounting can be 'taught', then, by any efforts to insure that a practitioner's work in these respects is exemplary. For instance, in small things: there should be a complete intolerance of dishonesty, misrepresentation, or action under conflict of interest in a firm as regards what a practitioner does even outside of an engagement—in such 'small matters' as the use of expense accounts; claiming of tax exemptions and deductions; and practices of billing." *(p. 169)*

~ "Culture in a firm is determined above all by the 'tone at the top'—the example set by management of moderation and integrity, but it is fostered of course by practices which draw attention to and reward action in which practitioners apparently sacrifice personal advantage for the sake of principle and probity." *(p. 169)*

1

Introduction

"BUSINESS ETHICS"... "ACCOUNTING ETHICS." Oddly enough, although accounting ethics would seem to be a branch of business ethics, these phrases tend to evoke different responses in non-professionals.

People like to joke that "business ethics" is an oxymoron—a contradiction in terms—because they presume that business cares only for the bottom line, to the neglect of ethics. On that presumption, business ethics looks to be an impossible endeavor, like squaring the circle.

But "accounting ethics" gets a different response. In this case, people sometimes wonder instead how it is that accountants *fail* to be ethical. They presume that accounting is about accuracy and integrity; that there can only be one correct number, as in mathematics. Aren't accountants the conscience of the business world, with critical eye and sharpened pencil at hand? So accounting ethics, or "ethics for accountants", looks like it should be an unnecessary endeavor, as if one were to speak of "military courage" or "logic for physicists." And contrary to that old accounting joke,[1] an accountant really cannot make

---

[1] Client to accountant: "What is two plus two?" Accountant: "What do you want it to be?"

two plus two equal five, without making himself look unprofessional and unethical. *Isn't accounting ethical because of the very nature of the profession?*

Both of these responses are of course oversimplified and incorrect. Success in business over the long haul depends upon good character and good ethical principles: hard work; honesty and plain dealing; an attitude of service; financial discipline; realism; good judgment; leadership; ease in working with and motivating others; concern for the good of the whole; and good relations with the community—to name just a few. Business ethics means reinforcing these good character traits and providing principles and case studies for dealing intelligently with difficult circumstances.

And since any profession consists of *professionals*, that is, human beings, who are open to the same failings that are evident in any human undertaking, accounting too needs ethical principles and guidance. This is especially true given that accounting is a relatively new profession (the first CPAs were recognized and awarded only at the beginning of the 20th century), and that the profession has changed so rapidly since the Second World War. Today much of accounting is about interpreting rules and making judgments. There often is no single correct answer. As a result, the nature of the profession, and its high ethical demands, can become less easy to follow. Add to this the multitude of changes in the business environment and law, and most accountants find themselves exposed to pressures and potential risks which require special attention and care. Thus, with regard to accounting ethics, it becomes especially necessary to rearticulate the ideals of the profession and to clarify how accountancy may be practiced with complete charity and integrity in new circumstances.

So accounting ethics turns out to be as necessary as business ethics is possible.

The recent crisis in accounting

Any sound approach to accounting ethics for today has to situate itself within the recent crisis in accounting. It's no news that the accounting profession is in crisis. But let's review the facts, to put things in perspective.

The profession has been roiled recently by some of the largest scandals in its history, especially Enron and WorldCom. The Enron scandal was the largest bankruptcy and fraud in the history of the world—but only for less than a year, until it was overtaken by the WorldCom debacle. Enron and WorldCom, although certainly noteworthy, were not isolated incidents but followed on the heels of a dozen other major scandals (such as Sunbeam, Xerox, and Waste Management, among others). And WorldCom has since been followed by additional scandals, such as accounting irregularities requiring Fannie Mae to restate its earnings over 2000-4, HealthSouth, and a developing major scandal involving AIG.

What only a decade earlier was the largest and one of the most prestigious of the big accounting firms, Arthur Andersen, was indicted for obstruction of justice following the Enron scandal. It was convicted, lost its ability to practice, and at a speed not even conceivable went out of business. Arthur Andersen, certainly one of the greatest accounting firms ever, now no longer exists.

In response to the Enron and WorldCom scandals, Congress passed the Sarbanes-Oxley Act of 2002, which President Bush quickly signed into law. Sarbanes-Oxley is the most comprehensive and expansive financial reform bill since the Great Depression, mandating significant changes in how internal accountants, internal auditors, and external auditors, carry on their work. Moreover, with regard to SEC registrants, Sarbanes-Oxley placed the accounting profession under a new, non-governmental regulatory agency, distinct from the profession itself, the Public Company Accounting Oversight Board (PCAOB).[2]

Naturally the vast majority of accountants have not been associated with these scandals or complicit in any irregularities. And it is true that there have been scandals and fraud throughout the history of business and accounting: "there is nothing new under the sun". All of these scandals had as their primary cause gross ethical lapses at the most senior levels of their organizations, and active efforts of management to mislead their auditors. Yet, although all this is true, given the facts rehearsed above, it would be a serious mistake not to conclude that the accounting

---

[2] The AICPA and Auditing Standards Board still function in a regulatory mode but are bound for any number of reasons to follow closely what the PCAOB enacts.

profession is in a crisis unique in its history. Most responsible observers recognize that this is so and hold furthermore that, in addition to the remedies provided by law, already mentioned, requiring reform 'from the outside', the crisis calls for a commensurate, serious response 'from the inside' of the profession itself.

> Naturally the vast majority of accountants have not been associated with these scandals or complicit in any irregularities. And it is true that there have been scandals and fraud throughout the history of business and accounting: "there is nothing new under the sun".

The President of the AICPA recently characterized the crisis as, in a word, the loss of "the perception of the audited financial statement as a clear picture window into a publicly traded company."[3]

Moroever, a consensus is forming on three distinct types of response that are needed. Call these the Three P's of Reform: (i) a return to *principle-based* rather than rule-based accounting; (ii) a rediscovery of how accounting should be practiced as a *profession* rather than a business; and (iii) the reclaiming of a certain *pride* in the profession, based on a correct self-image of the profession. Principles, Professionalism, and Pride. Let us look briefly at these in turn. We shall see that each of these types of reform implies a fundamental concern for ethics. Thus, *an attention to accounting ethics must be at the heart of any sound strategy of response to the current crisis in accounting.*

Principles-based accounting

Sherron Watkins described the attitude which prevailed in Enron as follows:

> In Houston, Enron Treasurer Jeff McMahon told me that Enron decided which rules got them the results they wanted, and the message to Andersen was, 'This is the way we're booking this. We won't change it unless you show us specifically where we've

---

[3] Barry C. Melancon, in a speech, "A New Accounting Culture," given at the invitation of the Yale School of Management, the Yale Club in New York City, September 4, 2002.

broken the rules.' McMahon spent over 2 years in our London office, and he said he could never get away with the same approach. In the U.K. they are more principle-based and, best of all, the auditor has the final say. If the auditor thinks the results are squirrelly and not representative of the true financial picture, then the auditor's decision holds—not the company's— if that company wants a clean opinion.[4]

At Enron, rules trumped principles rather than principles guiding the application of rules. And the external auditors allowed their judgment to be dictated in this way by the interests of the company, not by the requirements of the profession.

It follows that a reaffirmation of the primacy of principles over rules is essential to reform. The basic principles of accounting need to be identified and become well understood by practitioners, and then accountants need to acquire consistent habits of correctly placing principles above rules in the exercise of their professional judgment. Indeed, this is one of the fundamental approaches of the PCAOB. Its Chairman, William McDonough, recently explained that, "Our goal is to help practitioners better understand the principles underlying the standards and appreciate why it's important that they use judgment in applying them. We expect auditors and issuers alike to exercise judgment."[5]

The same line of thought is being followed within the profession. For instance, James H. Quigley, CEO for Deloitte & Touche, recently gave a talk to executives in Los Angeles on the topic of Sarbanes-Oxley compliance. He drew attention to various surveys which have shown that a majority of high-school students would contemplate cheating and defrauding others, if they would not be caught, and he suggested that accounting firms should play their part in reversing this attitude and helping to foster a "new age of accountability". He urged executives to

---

[4] In "Ethical Conflicts at Enron: Moral Responsibility in Corporate Capitalism", *California Review of Management*, vol. 45, no. 4, Summer 2003, pp. 6-19, Watkins' Petersen Lecture on Business Ethics at the Haas School of Business, U.C. Berkeley, January 30, 2003.
[5] November 10, 2004 address to the Financial Executives International meeting, New York City.

show "principle-centered leadership and a values-based approach to individual action." Quigley acknowledged that turning the tide would of course require "strong legislative measures", such as Sarbanes-Oxley, but he stressed that such legislation could be at best only part of a larger effort, which would additionally require *people of character, values-based individual involvement*, and *an enlightened corporate culture.*

As Quigley's remarks suggest, the return to principles-based accounting necessarily carries along with it a concern for ethics, values, character, and good culture. The reason is that the accounting profession can be regarded as something like a building or structure. The higher regions of this structure are particular judgments that a practitioner makes in the circumstances of daily work. These in a fashion rest upon practical guidance that the profession itself offers, in the form, for instance, of particular rulings by professional bodies such as the AICPA or PCAOB. These rulings in turn implement and rest upon more general rules. And these more general rules rest in turn upon principles, as upon a foundation.

But the principles of accounting are not yet the most basic level; they are the foundation, but not the solid ground or rock on which a foundation must rest. Principles need to be understood correctly and appropriately balanced against one another. Principles usually involve ideals, which need interpretation. The circumstances of a particular case also need to be taken into account. All of this requires judgment, as McDonough points out.[6] But judgment is inseparable from integrity and good professionalism, since no one who lacks integrity or professionalism can reliably exercise good judgment. Yet clearly integrity and professionalism are a matter of ethics. It follows that attention to ethics is a necessary part of the return to principle-based accounting. *There can be no principle-based accounting without attention to ethics.*

---

[6] As an illustration, see the AICPA 'Ethics Decision Tree' at http://www.aicpa.org/download/ethics/bai/decision_tree_bai.pdf. Ostensibly a simplified presentation, this Decision Tree is itself rather complicated and filled with qualifications and conditions. It's clear that an accountant who utilizes this tool should already possess a good, intuitive grasp of the ethical framework of the profession.

> Judgment is inseparable from integrity and good professionalism, since no one who lacks integrity or professionalism can reliably exercise good judgment.

A profession, not a business

Accounting is a profession, not a business. Later, in chapter four, we'll explain more carefully what makes a profession different from a business. Intuitively, a business provides a service to please a customer and ultimately at the bidding of a customer; a profession serves the public interest by adhering to an ideal.

Accounting is a profession which adheres to ideals of truthfulness and accuracy in order to support the trust that is necessary for flourishing business and healthy financial markets. This is well-captured in a speech by John Bogle, Founder of the Vanguard Group, when he served on the Independence Standards Board (since disbanded with the formation of the PCAOB). He first describes the societal need to which the profession of accounting answers:

> Sound securities markets require sound financial information. It is as simple as that. Investors require—and have a right to require—complete information about each and every security, information that fairly and honestly represents every significant fact and figure that might be needed to evaluate the worth of a corporation. Not only is accuracy required but, more than that, a broad sweep of information that provides every appropriate figure that a prudent, probing, sophisticated professional investor might require in the effort to decide whether a security should be purchased, held, or sold. Full disclosure. Fair disclosure. Complete disclosure. Those are the watchwords of the financial system that has contributed so much to our nation's growth, progress, and prosperity.[7]

Bogle then draws attention to what he calls "the pervasiveness of the societal trend of professions to become businesses", affecting law,

---

[7] The Seymour Jones Distinguished Lecture at the Vincent C. Ross Institute of Accounting Research Stern School of Business, New York University, New York, New York, October 16, 2000.

medicine, and financial services, and he claims that accounting finds itself under similar pressures. He speculates that the "high standards of the attestation profession" have served as something of a check on these pressures, but he warns that accounting nonetheless finds itself in danger of losing in part its integrity and independence:

> [O]ver the years, attestation has come to account for only about one-third of the $26 billion of revenues of today's "Big Five" accounting firms, with tax services accounting for one-quarter. The remainder, not far from one-half of revenues, is derived from consulting, management, and advisory services. The potential problem that arises from this trend, obviously, is that the desire to garner or retain a highly-lucrative consulting contract from an audit client could jeopardize the auditor's independence....
>
> It must also be clear that, whether or not the auditor has the backbone to maintain its independence under these circumstances, many management and consulting arrangements could easily be perceived as representing a new element in the relationship between auditor and corporation—a business relationship with a customer rather than a professional relationship with a client. Surely this issue goes to the very core of the central issue of philosophy that I expressed earlier: The movement of auditing from profession to business, with all the potential conflicts of interest that entails.

We'll see later in our case studies that Andersen adopted a business-partner role that apparently clouded its judgment and hindered it from performing its attest role correctly. Bogle's concerns were unfortunately amply vindicated.

Sarbanes-Oxley prohibits the relationships and conflicts of interest that Bogle highlights. Nonetheless, the law is not sufficient for fully correcting the problem, for two reasons. First, there is the problem of how in the first place the accounting profession might have allowed its nature as a profession to erode; such an internal change could not possibly be reversed simply by the passage and enforcement of a law. For instance, in the book, *Inside Arthur Andersen*, the authors describe what they call the 'partner purge' of 1992. A criterion was imposed on

Andersen partners of handling 20,000 billable hours per year. Those unable or unwilling to do so were asked to leave:

> The purge cut deeply, removing about 10 percent of the most conservative partners with traditional values, and increasing the value put on revenue generation through sales. Many of those removed were the most experienced individuals with a deep commitment to quality or were auditors with exceptional technical skills. They were good at conducting audits but not selling them. When Andersen lost these partners, the firm lost expertise through which quality was taught and learned....The purge also contributed to the destabilization of the delicate balance between youth and experience within the firm...With the partner purge, the role of the partners shifted to one aligned with management and sales.[8]

Clearly, a cultural shift of this kind within a firm could not be reversed simply through legislation. What would be needed, in addition, would be a change in the outlook of practitioners, toward a better understanding of and commitment to professionalism and all that it implies. The same thing of course applies as well to firms which did not have such a radical 'purge', but which still to some extent capitulated from within to the sorts of pressures that Bogle describes.

Second, there is the problem of 'the general fighting the last war'. Successful old generals often fail because they are fighting the last war, not the present war. Similarly, legislation often fails because it was designed to remedy bad practices from the past, not anticipating some new form of malfeasance. How can the accounting profession prevent a scandal from arising in the first place? How can it prevent the 'next' war from breaking out? Surely a firmer grasp of the nature of accounting as a profession is absolutely necessary for accountants today, precisely to guard against other, unforeseen ways in which the practitioners might go off track.

Professionalism is fundamentally an ethical orientation, implying integrity and adherence to high ideals. Thus, any reform that attempts

---

[8] Susan E. Squires, Cynthia J. Smith, Lorna McDougall, and William R. Yeack, *Inside Arthur Andersen: Shifting Values, Unexpected Consequences*, New York: Prentice Hall, 2003, p. 99.

to articulate, once again, the highest ideals of professionalism for an accountant, must necessarily pay careful attention to ethics. *There can be no true professionalism without attention to ethics.*

> Professionalism is an ethical orientation, implying integrity and adherence to high ideals. Any reform that attempts to articulate the highest ideals of professionalism for an accountant, must necessarily pay careful attention to ethics.

Pride in accounting

In his speech immediately following the passage of Sarbanes-Oxley, AICPA President Barry Melancon remarked:

> We are committed to rebuilding confidence in the financial markets and their institutions. We're committed to dramatically reducing the risk that future investors will fall prey to the kind of financial malfeasance that characterized Enron and WorldCom. And we are committed to something else as well: restoring pride in our profession. For us, it's personal.[9]

But how does one go about doing this? Melancon first acknowledges, as we have said, that there needs to be a reform from within the profession, and that externally mandated changes are insufficient:

> But let's recognize the challenge ahead: Reestablishing the perception of the audited financial statement as a clear picture window into a publicly traded company will not be achieved purely by legislation or regulation. No, the lead role must be played by all members of the profession. We must reach back to our core roots which earned us enormous respect as trusted advisers. We must reassert the heritage that made the accountant the professional in whom Americans confide their most confidential financial information and to whom they turn for honest advice.

---

[9] Barry C. Melancon, "A New Accounting Culture."

But this sort of reform involves articulating once again the ideals of the profession, and reasserting the true ethic, outlook, and culture of accountancy:

> What is needed is not just reform of the accounting laws, it is a rejuvenated accounting culture, both internally in corporate finance offices and externally in audit firms. The culture must build upon the profession's traditional values, such as rigorous commitment to integrity, a passion for getting it right, a commitment to rules—not just to their letter, but their spirit, and zero tolerance for those who break them. These values are the commitment of all of the 350,000 CPAs who are members of the AICPA across this country. We are determined to restore the image of the accounting profession and rebuild the legacy we will pass on to the next generation of accountants.

Clearly what Melancon talks about here—integrity; a passion for getting it right; the profession's 'traditional values'—are all a matter of accounting ethics. Therefore, *there can be no new accounting culture without a turn to accounting ethics.*

Virtue-based ethics

In this book, we provide a virtue-based approach to accounting ethics. "There is a need for virtue in accounting, because the virtues enable accountants to resist client and commercial pressures that may result between an accountant's obligation to a client or employer and public interest considerations."[10] In a virtue-based approach to the profession, one first identifies the distinctive 'function' or purpose of accounting. We maintain that the function of accounting is to enable the trust that is required for thriving business and sound financial markets. Next one considers what traits an accountant should have, in order to carry out this distinctive function well. We therefore go on to explain what the traits of objectivity, integrity, and independence are, and how these are the 'virtues' of an accountant.

---

[10] S. Mintz, "Virtue Ethics and Accounting Education", *Issues in Accounting Education* 10 (Fall): 247-267, p. 247.

A virtue-based approach to ethics looks upon an agent as not simply an intellect or mind, but rather as a whole person, with loyalties and commitments ('heart'), interests, and desires, who responds in characteristic ways to incentives and to his or her surrounding culture. A virtue-based approach is practical. It pays attention not simply to what principles or rules are relevant to ethics, but also to questions such as: How can an accountant take care not to let his ethical reasoning be deflected or subverted by emotions such as vanity, or self-interested motives such as greed? What should an accountant's character be like, so that he reliably acts in an upright manner? To what ideals should an accountant be passionately committed, in order to persevere in acting rightly over the long haul? Because a virtue-based approach is in this way practical, it gives useful direction for teaching and inculcating ethics, as we explain below in chapter 7.

> A virtue-based approach to ethics looks upon an agent as not simply an intellect or mind, but rather as a whole person, with loyalties and commitments ('heart'), interests, and desires, who responds in characteristic ways to incentives and to his or her surrounding culture.

Virtue-based reasoning is attractive because it is similar to sound managerial and administrative reasoning generally. It matches very closely the ways of thinking with which business people will already be familiar. It has also proven to be well suited to explaining the inherently ethical nature of a profession, as it is used widely and with success for ethical education in medicine and law. "The reason for the indispensability of virtue ethics", writes a leading medical ethicist, Edmund Pellegrino, M.D., "is the ineradicability of the moral agent in the moral life."

All principles, duties and rules of ethics must ultimately be expressed in the moral life of the living human agent. How duties, rules, obligations, sentiments, etc. are acted upon, interpreted, given weight, put into priority and with what intention or motives, are all shaped by the character of the moral

agent. The agent, therefore, cannot be left out of the judgment
of the moral status of any particular human act.[11]

Pellegrino speaks of the "revival" of virtue-based ethics in medicine and attributes this to the prior "dominance of principle-based ethics which some consider too abstract or limited in its interpretation of the professional life".   On this approach, the physician's relationship with the patient "could not be a contract or a commodity transaction. It is a covenant or trust, a special kind of promise to serve those who require her expertise. Suppression of self-interest would be a natural corollary of a virtue-oriented physician."

> A physician's relationship with the patient could not be a contract or a commodity transaction. It is a covenant or trust, a special kind of promise to serve.

A physician trained in this approach, Pellegrino remarks, acquires an outlook such that he refuses to "compromise his personal or professional integrity for political, economic, or social advancement."

This book represents some first steps toward adapting such an approach in the education of accountants as professionals. In opting for a virtue-based approach to ethics, we particularly want to avoid both the 'cafeteria selection' and 'values clarification' approaches to accounting ethics adopted by some authors. We do not believe that ethics is suitably taught by providing practitioners with a variety of speculative ethical theories (act-utilitarianism, rule-utilitarianism, deontology) and then considering how different theories yield different results. Such an approach, we believe, contributes to an attitude of moral relativism which we regard as corrosive to principled conduct. We think it better, rather, to attempt to draw out naturally, *from the ethical code already accepted by the profession*, those fundamental principles that explain this code. Furthermore, we do not suppose that sound ethical principles are already somehow implicit in everyone, so that they can be reliably arrived at by a process of 'clarification'. We make no pretense of neutrality. Let us be

---

[11] Edmund D. Pellegrino, M.D., "Professionalism, Profession, and the Virtues of the Good Physician", *Mount Sinai Journal of Medicine*, 69, 2002, 378-384, p. 380.

clear: in our view, neutrality in ethical matters is neither attainable nor desirable. For instance, we positively support and aim at integrity in the profession, without qualification or hesitation. Accounting ethics, as we see it, is therefore not a matter of mere 'values clarification' from a neutral perspective, but rather it is the attempt to state principles which an intelligent practitioner of upright character would set down and regard as authoritative for the discipline. This attempt may be imperfect or even incorrect in places, and yet it is important to attempt it, for all that. A 'risky' attempt to state sound ethical principles, we consider, is better than a perfectly 'safe' attempt which affirms everything or nothing at all.

The purpose of this book

At first glance, ethics seems useless. What does it do? What special expertise does it confer? What power does it give to anyone? But ethics, like philosophy, in reality governs everything that we do, because we are intelligent beings, and we live by the *understanding* that we have of things. A comparison may be drawn with a sport such as golf: frequently some apparently useless idea or image, provided by an instructor, proves to be the key that one was looking for to make new progress. In fact the best instructors seem to focus on basic concepts rather than particular techniques.

"It is foolish, generally speaking," G.K. Chesterton wrote, "for a philosopher to set fire to another philosopher in Smithfield Market because they do not agree in their theory of the universe. That was done very frequently in the last decadence of the Middle Ages, and it failed altogether in its object. But there is one thing that is infinitely more absurd and unpractical than burning a man for his philosophy. This is the habit of saying that his philosophy does not matter." Chesterton goes on to say:

> But there are some people, nevertheless—and I am one of them—who think that the most practical and important thing about a man is still his view of the universe. We think that for a landlady considering a lodger, it is important to know his income, but still more important to know his philosophy. We think that for a general about to fight an enemy, it is important

> to know the enemy's numbers, but still more important to know the enemy's philosophy. We think the question is not whether the theory of the cosmos affects matters, but whether in the long run, anything else affects them.[12]

We agree with Chesterton and hold that what is fundamentally important for a practitioner is the 'philosophy' of the accounting profession that he or she adopts, and this will be a matter of 'ethics', in the broad sense.

An accountant's 'philosophy' is important for achieving unity of life. One needs to consider: Is accountancy a profession that can serve as the organizing principle of a worthwhile human life? Compare how one regards physicians or professors. We know what it means to be a true healer dedicated to health; we see, likewise, that there is a complete, admirable way of life bound up with being a 'scholar'. Is there similarly an admirable way of life which goes along with being a professional accountant? We do not mean, for instance, a life of fastidiousness and accuracy, as in popular stereotypes and caricatures, but rather a life imbued with such traits as integrity and uprightness. "Think straight, talk straight" was the motto of Arthur Andersen, and it indicated a much respected approach to life in general:

> "Think straight talk straight" was the principle on which Arthur E. Andersen built his accounting practice. It was a phrase his mother had taught him. It became the firm's motto and appeared on many internal documents. The commitment to integrity and a systematic, planned approach to work is what he offered his clients, and this brand of audit proved attractive to both corporate clients and investors.[13]

---

[12] G.K. Chesterton, *Heretics*, "Introductory Remarks on the Importance of Orthodoxy", available online at: http://www.dur.ac.uk/martin.ward/gkc/books/heretics/ch1.html. The website adds this note: Heretics was copyrighted in 1905 by the John Lane Company. This electronic text is derived from the twelfth (1919) edition published by the John Lane Company of New York City and printed by the Plimpton Press of Norwood, Massachusetts. The text carefully follows that of the published edition (including British spelling).

[13] *Inside Arthur Andersen*, pp. 31-32. See also Arthur Andersen & Co., 1974, *The First Sixty Years: 1913-1973*.

Accountants as professionals understandably want to set a good example, and be of service, outside the narrow confines of their discipline. Accountants should have a distinctive and admirable presence among friends and in their communities. But this can be accomplished only if they discover or rediscover, one by one, and on a personal basis, the ethical appeal and foundations of their discipline.

> Is accountancy a profession that can serve as the organizing principle of a worthwhile human life? Is there an admirable way of life which goes along with being a professional accountant?

But apart from these very basic reasons for studying accounting ethics, there is a very practical reason as well, namely, that sound ethics on average, and in the long run, leads to business success. This point is well-illustrated by a story told by George O. May, which it is worthwhile recounting in full:

A good many years ago—as a matter of fact, in 1899—owing to the death of one of the senior partners, I was called upon to settle with an important New York banker the form of a certificate for use in connection with a prospectus. As the issue was to be made on both sides of the Atlantic, it was planned to print the accountants' certificate in the prospectus as was and is customary in England.

The profits of the company showed a fairly steady decline over a period of ten years except that in 1898, owing to the Spanish-American War, they rose considerably to a point higher than the average of the ten years. The banker desired the certificate to show only the average for the ten years and the profits for the last year. I demurred to this suggestion on two grounds: first, that it was contrary to the practice of my firm to show only averages where the profits for separate years were readily ascertainable; and, secondly, that the information proposed to be given would create a natural but erroneous impression as to the trend of profits.

The discussion became difficult, and it was indicated that if we adhered to the position I had taken there would be no possibility of any similar differences with that particular banker in the future. However, I refused to modify the stand I had taken and was supported by the senior partner, with the result that no certificate was printed in the prospectus, but a statement was made by the banker on his own responsibility. I felt that I was right, but I could not fail to be conscious of the fact that my first important interview with a banker had not been a success and promised to result in the loss of an important client.

There was, however, a sequel. Some six months later, the same banker was contemplating the purchase of a business and desired a full and reliable report on its operations. His lawyers approached the firm saying that while he still thought we were entirely wrong in the stand we had taken six months earlier, he believed that we had taken it in perfect good faith and that the incident should not, therefore, be a bar to friendly relations between us. They thereupon gave us instructions to make the investigation, and further intimated that the banker desired that I should personally take charge of it; and I may add that the banker is today a valued client of the firm.

This sequel made the whole incident one of the most helpful of my experiences, and I hope it may also be of service in encouraging those of you who may be about to start practice, or are in the early days of practice, to take a firm stand for sound ethical principles, which I am sure will ultimately tend to bring you professional success as well as a consciousness of professional integrity.[14]

---

[14] "The Accountant and the Investor" in George Oliver May, *Twenty-Five Years of Accounting Responsibility, 1911-1936, Essays and Discussions,* edited by Bishop Carleton Hunt. Price, Waterhouse, & Co, 1936.

The intended audience of this book

In introducing the story given above, May observes that "[t]he young accountant may find it hard to take the first stand for the principles that have been suggested for his observance, but he will find this is essentially a case in which 'it is the first step that costs'." In the same spirit, this book is intended for students of accounting, and for practitioners who are at the beginning of their career. We firmly believe that the exposition of the ideals and principles of accounting ethics, as provided in this text, will help provide needed assistance in taking that 'first step that costs.'

But the book is also intended as a guide to seasoned internal accountants, internal auditors, and external auditors, who wish to arrive at a deeper understanding of the profession to which they have already committed years of their life and long hours of service.

Finally, the book should be a useful guide, also, for executives and professionals who deal regularly with accountants, and who wish to gain a good intuitive grasp of the outlook of an accountant, and of the standards that govern an accountant's work. This would include CFOs, members of audit and finance committees, and investors.

Outline of the book

We begin the book by making a fairly detailed argument, in chapter two, that an accountant, in the exercise of his or her professional judgment, cannot rely solely on accounting rules, but must at every point make implicit reference to deeper principles of accounting. It then becomes clear that there can be no intelligent recourse to principles, without an implicit reliance, as well, upon the ethical ideals of accounting. It follows that any accountant, willy-nilly, relies upon ethical considerations. *Ethics is not an option but a practical necessity in the exercise of professional judgment.* The point of this argument is to convince even the most 'hard-headed' devotee of technical principles in accounting that a consideration of accounting ethics is unavoidable. If it is unavoidable, it should be done right, and that is what we hope to achieve in the rest of the book.

> Ethics is not an option but a practical necessity in the exercise of professional judgment.

We therefore move on, in chapter three, to give some basic concepts and principles of virtue-based ethics. We bring in speculative theories of ethics, such as utilitarianism and deontology, largely to provide a contrast, but we also give some basic arguments as to why a virtue-based approach is to be preferred over these. We explain how virtues are to be understood, as traits that equip someone with a certain task to carry out that task well. We also introduce and discuss some other foundational notions of ethics, such as 'common good' and 'law.'

With these foundational notions in hand, we then proceed, in chapter four, to apply the virtue-based approach to the profession of accounting. We identify the distinctive task or contribution to society of an accountant. We hold that this is the trust needed for a flourishing market economy. From this starting point, we ask what traits an accountant needs to have, in order to carry out this task well. Reasoning in this way, we show how it is possible to arrive at the basic principles contained within the Code of Professional Ethics of the AICPA and similar ethical codes formulated by professional associations of accountants. We discuss also the nature of a profession, and why it is that accounting qualifies as a profession rather than merely a business.

In each of chapters two through four we conclude our discussion with an important legal case, in which the ideas of the chapter are illustrated. There are three reasons for this. First, the legal case allows us to present a detailed case with its own distinctive circumstances and incidents. This is important because all ethical deliberation, because it is practical, is ultimately directed to particular cases, not general principles. The reader therefore gets 'practice' in looking at particular cases in the light of general principles. Second, the legal cases show nicely the interplay of law and ethics. It is sometimes said that law is 'ethically neutral' and should ideally not be used to 'impose a morality'. But nothing is further from the truth. All law contains implicit ethical ideals, principles, and rankings. This becomes explicit in opinions of the court based on law. That law and ethics are thus intertwined then becomes a further argument, if any were needed, of the great practical importance of ethics for accounting. Third, the legal cases we look at are worth knowing in their own right; they have set down precedents which have subsequently affected the professional work of accountants.

After these expository chapters, we follow with chapters on the Enron and WorldCom scandals, showing how these cases illustrate and verify the view of accounting ethics which we had developed in earlier chapters. We give an anatomy of the fraud, which should help the reader to understand how the frauds were accomplished, and the role played by internal accountants and auditors, and external auditors. We aim to answer the question, "How can good professionals do bad things?", while drawing general lessons that are practically useful. Although the Enron and WorldCom cases have received extensive media attention, we believe that, still, that attention has been relatively superficial. The 'true story' of these cases and the 'true lessons' to be learned remain widely unappreciated, even to practitioners who suppose that they know these cases well enough.

Finally, in a concluding chapter we discuss the ancient question, "Can ethics be taught?". Here we exhibit the great strength and richness of a virtue-based approach to accounting ethics, since we are able to derive various concrete suggestions for ethics education for accountants and for the reform of the profession.

"We're looking forward to reclaiming our profession's heritage as a bedrock of business integrity and continuing our historic role as trusted advisers to businesses of all sizes and protectors of the public interest," AICPA President Barry Melancon said, at the conclusion of his speech quoted above, "It will not be easy. But we are committed to it. We are committed to moving forward. We will rebuild trust in our profession brick by brick." Earlier we likened the accounting profession to a building built upon a foundation of principles resting on the solid rock of ethics. As professional associations and regulatory agencies are hard at work, cementing the bricks, we hope in this book to carry out the complementary work of uncovering the solid basis of accounting ethics.

2

From Rules to Principles

ALL RIGHT, THEN: SUPPOSE YOU ARE A SCEPTIC about the value of ethics. Perhaps you are a hard-nosed practitioner who revels in the technical details of an engagement. Or perhaps you are a student, having a hard enough time becoming proficient in the field. Maybe you think that "ethics is for someone else", but not for you. The point of this chapter is to convince you otherwise.

Here is our argument. Imagine a skilled and intelligent practitioner who was intent on avoiding the study of accounting ethics altogether. He has studied the relevant rules and rulings of professional boards. He knows the relevant facts. He thinks it is enough to master the rules and put them into practice, given the facts. If so, then he has no need of studying ethics more deeply.

But it can be demonstrated—we contend—that his mastery of the rules will not be sufficient. He will need to be relying constantly on good judgment, and appealing frequently to implicit ideals. Yet, if this is granted, then it is clear that he is inevitably caught up in considerations that are in the domain of ethics. Ethics is in practice unavoidable. An accountant cannot but appeal to ethical notions, even in his ordinary work as an accountant.

But if ethical reflection is inevitable, then it should be done well. And the point of the rest of the book, following this opening argument, is to illustrate how it can be carried out well.

Rules are not enough

Rules are not sufficient for the good practice of accounting. To see this, consider the following fact pattern as regards possible conflicts of interest. We choose it as a simple, everyday example; you may regard it as an instance which represents the sort of thing that can come up regularly.

> Alison, Bill, and Cathy are members of Accurate Accounting, LLP, and are engaged to audit Classic Car Company of New England.
>> • Alison has a relative who has at various times *invested* in Classic Car Company.
>> • Bill has a relative who is an *employee* of Classic Car Company.
>> • For part of her work on the engagement, Cathy uses the services of a *consulting company*, which employs a relative of an employee of Classic Car Company.
> Would the independence of Alison, Bill, or Cathy be considered impaired? What would we need to know in order to decide this?

Will an appeal to the relevant rules suffice to decide these matters? A practitioner might consult, for instance, the interpretations provided by the AICPA of the standard of Independence in its Code of Professional Conduct. These interpretations aim to identify the usual sorts of conflict of interest for practitioners and render decisions about them. ET §101.11 provides various rules that are relevant to these cases. Applying those rules to the present case, we may determine:

As regards Alison, her independence would be regarded as impaired if four conditions were satisfied:

(i) If the investment of Alison's relative were *material* to the relative; and

(ii) If the relative had invested during the time of the engagement or when Accurate Accounting expressed its opinion; and

(iii) If Alison *knew* of the relative's investment; and

(iv) If the relative were Alison's spouse or dependent.

If all of these conditions were satisfied, then Alison's independence would be considered impaired.

As regards Bill, his independence would be regarded as impaired if two conditions were jointly satisfied:

(i) If the relative had a position at Classic Car that was audit sensitive; and

(ii) If the relative were Bill's spouse or dependent.

As regards Cathy, her independence would be regarded as impaired (indirectly so, on the grounds that the consulting firm on which she depended would not be regarded as independent) if three conditions were satisfied:

(i) If Cathy had relied upon the consulting company for a significant part of the engagement; and

(ii) If the relative of the employee of the consulting company, who works for Classic Car, were a spouse or dependent; and

(iii) If that relative who works for Classic Car had significant influence in that company or were involved in audit-sensitive work in that company.

These considerations, although admittedly complex, are familiar and not difficult. They are standard conditions that need to be taken into account in order to make decisions in these sorts of cases about independence.

However, we are not so much interested in the rules, and in these conditions, but rather in a fact about this appeal to rules, which is obvious once noted, but which is not unimportant for all that. The important fact is that *this appeal to rules, which we had hoped would decide the matter for us, is not sufficient on its own to decide our difficulty*. And this is something of a surprising fact, given the complexity of these rules, and the detail to which these particular concerns about conflict of interest have been worked out. If rules are insufficient to decide a commonplace and relatively simple case like this, then we can be assured that they are insufficient generally.

Our appeal to rules is insufficient on its own for a variety of identifiable reasons. It is useful to articulate these reasons and examine them individually:

1. Rules state only *necessary*, not *sufficient* conditions: they are essentially open-ended and cannot take into account all possible cases.

2. Rules make use of terms that require *interpretation*. We cannot indefinitely clarify rules with further rules: at some point we must rely upon good judgment in interpreting the rules.

3. We must appeal to *idealizations* in order to interpret the rules: rules are useless if used by someone who lacks a good sense of these idealizations.

4. Even to care about interpreting the rules correctly, we need to place our getting them right over considerations of self-interest, convenience, comfort, and inclination. Rules are useless except for someone with the correct motivation.

5. Rules on their own are *unmanageable*: we can practically speaking make sense of them, remember them, and use them as guides for action, only in relation to the principles they are meant to embody.

6. We cannot be said actually to follow a rule, unless we can *recognize when our actions are in conformity* with that rule; yet our successfully recognizing this is itself not contained in the rule, and it must presuppose some other disposition.

Let us consider each of these points in turn. Taken together, they establish that *rules are for principles, not principles for rules*.

---

1. Rules can state only necessary, not sufficient conditions: they are essentially open-ended and cannot take into account all possible cases.

By a 'necessary condition' we mean a 'that without which not'. It is a 'requirement', or a *sine qua non*. We call such a condition 'necessary' because, if it is not satisfied, then that which requires it cannot exist. To get clear about this, consider the following claim:

(S1) A good source of electricity is a necessary condition for a washing machine to work.

That is: without a good source of electricity, the machine will not work. Electricity, then, is a 'necessary condition' of washing one's clothes in a washing machine.

In contrast, a sufficient condition is something that suffices to bring a thing into existence or realize it. Once we bring about a sufficient condition for a thing, then immediately we bring about that thing as well. A sufficient condition implies or guarantees the existence of that of which it is a condition. Consider, for example, this claim:

(S2) A good source of electricity is not a sufficient condition for washing your clothes.

This is true since, after all, the machine might be broken, in which case it will not be enough simply to have a good source of electricity.

Rules about conflicts of interest, such as the AICPA interpretations cited above, give only necessary conditions for an accountant's independence, not sufficient conditions. They give requirements of independence; they state what must be the case, if a practitioner is to be independent; they identify some of the things (usually the most salient or most common things) that cannot be lacking in an independent practitioner. But such rules do not provide sufficient conditions. No matter how complicated or detailed the rule, it remains a possibility that a practitioner satisfies all the stated rules, but still lacks independence— because (say) there exists a conflict of interest, which arises out of circumstances not envisaged by or articulated in the rules.

A necessary condition: a requirement.
A sufficient condition: a guarantee.

This is an extremely important point. It follows from it that the following is a fallacy:

(S3) I followed all the relevant rules, therefore I acted
properly.

The rules, as we noted, do not express sufficient conditions of proper
conduct; thus, to follow the rules is not itself a guarantee of propriety.

It is instructive that, immediately following its statement of rules,
the AICPA Code adds the following important reminder:

(S4) "Members must be aware that it is impossible to
enumerate all circumstances wherein the appearance of
a member's independence might be questioned by a
third party. For example, a member's relationship with a
cohabitant may be equivalent to that of a spouse."

We can amend the rule to take this into account, of course, but that by
no means changes the basic nature of the rule.

> **2. Rules make use of terms that require interpretation. We cannot
> indefinitely clarify rules with further rules: at some point we must rely
> upon good judgment in interpreting the rules.**

Look again at the statements above of the relevant rules. The rules
make use of the terms such as 'material', 'significant', 'substantial',
'audit-sensitive', and so on, which themselves require intelligent
interpretation.

For instance, Bill's independence is affected if his spouse's position
at Classic Car is 'audit-sensitive'. Is there some rule that clarifies what
an 'audit-sensitive' position is? Yes, the AICPA code indeed provides a
rule to help us interpret its rule:

(S5) "In general, a person's activities would be
considered audit-sensitive if such activities are normally
an element of or subject to significant internal
accounting controls."

But note that this further rule contains an important qualification: it
holds only "in general" (or "for the most part"). That is, it is not meant
to rule out other cases, where an employee's activities are not "normally
an element of or subject to significant internal accounting controls" yet
are audit-sensitive nonetheless. (It is not difficult to contrive such

cases.) Furthermore, this rule as well contains terms that require interpretation: it refers to activities that 'normally' are an element of internal accounting controls, where these controls are furthermore 'significant'. But what counts as being 'normally' an element? What counts as a 'significant' control? If we tried to define these terms with further rules, we would find that terms requiring interpretation would crop up once again, in our rules for understanding rules about rules.

It will not help to try to enumerate cases, because such an enumeration could not possibly be exhaustive. As the AICPA code adds:

> (S6) "For example, the following positions, which are not intended to be all-inclusive, would normally be considered audit-sensitive: cashier; internal auditor; accounting supervisor; purchasing agent; or inventory warehouse supervisor."

The list is illustrative only, not exhaustive (note that it uses 'or', not 'and' to link the items together). The practitioner must therefore grasp the sort of thing that is meant by the items on the list and be prepared to recognize, as similar, an indefinite number of cases which are not however enumerated.

Because rules are in this way incomplete, we therefore reach the following extremely important conclusion: *It is in principle impossible to capture in rules everything that is contained in an ethical principle or ideal.*

> No ethical principle or ideal can be entirely captured in a set of rules.

It follows, therefore, that a good practitioner must always use good judgment in arriving at a sound interpretation of accounting rules.

3. We must appeal to idealizations in order to interpret rules: rules are useless if employed by someone who lacks a good sense of these idealizations.

Very frequently, in order to interpret those open-ended terms contained in a rule, we need to appeal to what an ideally 'reasonable person' or 'impartial observer' would judge to be the case.

For instance, in (S4) above it was stated that various relationships besides being a spouse or dependent can affect the independence or perceived independence of a practitioner. Suppose for instance that Bill has a cousin who works at Classic Car. Ordinarily, the relationship of cousin would be considered sufficiently remote as not to affect independence. But suppose that, in this case, Bill and his cousin grew up together and regard themselves as 'best friends' and akin to brothers. Suppose that in many other contexts Bill and his cousin have collaborated on business enterprises and initiatives. Should Bill's relationship to his cousin, then, be taken to affect his independence? How should Bill decide? The relevant rule on its own gives no answer: the relevant rule mentions only spouses and dependents.

What we need to do, in that case, is to appeal to a kind of idealization of the rule, as interpreted by an ideal interpreter. The idealized rule would be something like this:

> (S6) Independence is affected if a practitioner has a
> relationship to an employee which is close enough that it
> might tend to influence or sway his or her judgment.

But whether *that* idealized rule is satisfied is something that we judge by imagining how a reasonable observer, with knowledge of the relevant facts, and with a good grasp of human nature and how people typically act, would look upon the situation. What we would need to consider is: Would such an observer conclude that Bill's judgment was in danger of being swayed, or that someone looking on might be confident that Bill's judgment had not been swayed? Thus, as the AICPA code remarks (in the sentences immediately following the passage we had quoted as (S4)):

> (S7) "In addition, in situations involving assessment of
> the association of any relative or dependent person with
> a client, members must consider whether the strength of
> personal and business relationships between the
> member and the relative or dependent person, in
> conjunction with the specified association with the

client, would lead a reasonable person aware of all the facts, who took into consideration normal strength of character and normal behavior under such circumstances, to conclude that the situation poses an unacceptable threat to the member's objectivity and appearance of independence".

But how do we decide what a 'reasonable person aware of all the facts' would decide? In many cases a practitioner can seek the advice of an experienced and detached colleague. But even in that case he or she would have to rely on his or her own sense of whether that colleague had given sensible advice after all. Thus:

> The interpretation of any rule requires an appeal to how a reasonable person would judge or view things.

There is no escaping the conclusion, then, that *to interpret rules correctly requires that we ourselves have good sense; experience; familiarity; and reasonability about those matters with which the rules deal.*

4. Even to care about interpreting the rules correctly, we need to place our getting them right over considerations of self-interest, convenience, comfort, and inclination. Rules are useless except for someone with the correct motivation.

So far we have been looking at various ways in which, from the nature of the case, 'rules are not enough.' A rule only roughly circumscribes an area in which correct conduct is found; it cannot exactly point out correct conduct. No rule can cover in advance all possible cases in human action: a rule must remain open-ended. A rule must be interpreted, and we need to use good sense in interpreting it.

But an even more basic insufficiency of a rule is—obviously—that people need to be committed to following the rule, and this commitment itself cannot come from the rule. Why? Well, how might we construct a rule that tried to be the source of concern for itself?

Suppose that we added to a rule an imperative enjoining commitment, "And you must be committed to following this rule!" For instance:

> (S8) "A member should refuse an engagement with an enterprise if his or her spouse does audit-sensitive work for the enterprise—and a member must be committed to following this rule!"

Clearly, the clause enjoining commitment is itself part of the rule; hence it has force only if someone is *already* committed to following the rule. It adds no additional force on its own.

Furthermore, to follow the rule seems less important than the good of independence, which the rule is meant to safeguard. Thus, what the first part of the rule enjoins (avoiding something that compromises independence) is more important than what the second part of the rule enjoins (simply following the rule). So anyone who lacked commitment to the first part of the rule, which concerns the more important goal, could hardly acquire that sort of commitment on account of the second part of the rule, which concerns a lesser goal.

Neither would it help to add a separate rule enjoining commitment to *all of the rules*. Suppose that at the end of the AICPA Code of Professional Conduct one were to add a rule that stated:

> (S9) Members are to follow all of the rules in this Code.

Then we would have the same problem as before: since (S9) is a part of the Code, it can add no force to the Code; and in any case what the rules of the Code enjoin is more important than what (S9) enjoins.[15]

> To follow a rule presupposes a commitment which cannot be captured in rules.

No doubt it is with a view to this difficulty that the AICPA Code at the start appeals, not to a rule, but to the free and voluntary commitment of practitioners to abide by the standards and principles of accounting. In fact the very first lines of the Code are as follows:

---

[15] Compare Rule 3100 recently promulgated by PCAOB: "A registered public accounting firm and its associated persons shall comply with all applicable auditing and related professional standards"—apparently a rule enjoining the following of the rules.

(S10)   "Membership in the American Institute of Certified Public Accountants is voluntary. By accepting membership, a certified public accountant assumes an obligation of self-discipline above and beyond the requirements of laws and regulations."

Note the words: "beyond the requirements of laws and regulations."[16]

> **5. Rules on their own are unmanageable: practically speaking, we can make sense of them, remember them, and use them as guides for action, only if we understand them in relation to the principles they are meant to embody.**

The cases of Alison, Bob, and Cathy sketched above are different from one another. Alison has a close relative who invests in a client company; Bob has a similar relative who is an employee; Cathy employs an agent who has a relative in the company, whose activities would be related in a special way to an audit Cathy might perform.   How do we collect these and other similar instances together, as variations on a similar theme? Of course, we take them all to be illustrations of how 'independence' might be diminished.

And yet this ability to collect particular particulars and treat them as instances of the same thing is important. We unify *cases* relative to a *rule*, and we in turn unify *rules* relative to *principles* or *ideals* which the rules are meant to safeguard.

> We unify various cases only by seeing them as expressions of the same ideal.

If we lacked a grasp of the relevant principles and ideals, each rule would stand on its own, in isolation. It would be 'meaningless'—something to follow simply as a kind of game or challenge.

---

[16] Above all *laws*, even? Are we meant to think that the obligation that is freely accepted by a professional accountant is higher than state and federal law? Presumably, yes. As we shall see in chapter three below, a profession is defined essentially by a commitment of that sort.

> 6. We cannot be said actually to follow a rule, unless we can recognize when our actions are in conformity with that rule; yet our successfully recognizing this is itself not contained in the rule, and it must presuppose some other disposition.

Here is an instance of what we mean, from science. Suppose a student is doing a science experiment and wants to follow the rule, "Heat the mixture until it reaches 50 degrees Centigrade." He therefore begins to heat the mixture, then places a Centigrade thermometer in the mixture, and he removes the heat from the mixture when the thermometer reads 50 degrees.

The student would be unable to follow the rule without a thermometer. He needs some way of checking that his behavior conforms to the rule. But, more than this, he has to have some assurance that the thermometer is accurate. Perhaps he has purchased it from a reputable company. Or perhaps to verify the thermometer's accuracy he performs a test, such as placing it in boiling water, to make sure that in those circumstances it reads 100 degrees, as it should.

Suppose that when he places the thermometer in boiling water, to check its accuracy, he finds that it reads 95 degrees. It would be likely, then, that the thermometer was in error; yet the student could not immediately be confident of that. He would need to investigate more, taking steps to see if he cannot remove the ostensible error. Perhaps the thermometer was inaccurate, or perhaps the water was impure, or something else interfered with its reading.

The student's reliance on the thermometer, and his being disposed to investigate if he had reason to think that it was erroneous—all of this is presupposed in his using the thermometer to check whether the mixture has indeed reached 50 degrees Centigrade. That is to say, *to use some measurement or criterion to verify that one has followed a rule, is to presuppose that one has taken reasonable and sufficient precautions to insure that one is correct in thinking that one's behavior thus conforms to the rule.* It must be reasonable for a rule-follower to rely on those instruments and measures for self-checking, on which he or she does rely.

A similar condition holds for accountants. In any task of accountancy or auditing, this condition is commonly accepted and is called 'diligence', 'reasonable diligence', 'due diligence', or 'due care'.

Here are some examples from the AICPA book of professional standards, where this condition is referred to:

> (S11) In conducting a review, "...if the accountant becomes aware that information coming to his attention is incorrect, incomplete, or otherwise unsatisfactory, he should perform the additional procedures he deems necessary to achieve limited assurance that there are no material modifications that should be made to the financial statements in order for the statements to be in conformity with generally accepted accounting principles" (AR §100.30).

Of course the demands of reasonable diligence increase with the nature of a practitioner's services and in proportion to the degree of assurance claimed (compilation, review, audit). This is what is meant by due diligence: diligence in proportion to the significance of the claim and the risk of error.

> Due diligence: verification undertaken in proportion to the importance of success and the risk of error.

Proportionate diligence is everywhere presupposed by the Code of Professional Conduct. Consider for instance Cathy in our example. When she makes use of the services of a consulting agency, she should do so on the condition that this does not affect her independence. Her independence might be affected, if there were some close relationship between a member of that consulting agency and a member of the client company. To what extent, then, is she responsible for checking to be sure that there is not such a relationship? She should use the discretion and diligence that is required given the task at hand and the circumstances:

> (S12) "The member should make a reasonable inquiry to determine whether such relationships exist, and if they do, careful consideration should be given to

whether the financial interests in question would lead a reasonable observer to conclude that the specified relationships pose an unacceptable threat to the member's independence."

It is worth noting that the notion of 'due diligence' in following a rule corresponds to what in moral philosophy and law is known as 'culpable ignorance'. Culpable ignorance is blameworthy ignorance; it is a state of not knowing what you were capable of knowing and what you should have taken the pains to come to know. Culpable ignorance is ignorance that is an exception to the ordinary rule that 'ignorance of particulars exculpates, but ignorance of general principles does not': culpable ignorance involves particulars, but it is blameworthy because, if the agent had taken reasonable or due care, he would not have been ignorant.

An example: a man runs over with his car what looks to be a pile of clothing on the road, but it turns out later that the 'pile of clothing' was actually a drunken homeless man. When he is indicted for manslaughter, he claims: "I'm not to blame, because I didn't know that it was a man." But everything hinges on whether he should have known that it was a man. And whether he should have known, depends upon whether, if he had taken due care, he would have discovered that it was a man.

> Culpable ignorance: you were capable of knowing something, and you should have taken pains to come to know it.

What counts as due care, in such a case, will vary with context and circumstances. If the 'pile of clothes' is in the middle of a major road far from dwellings, then it might be reasonable to presume that it was not a homeless person; if the 'pile' is on a city road, in a neighborhood where there are many homeless, then it would be reasonable to suspect that it might be a homeless person—and not to drive over the 'pile' until one had assurance that it definitely was not.

Rules require principles and character

It is clear, then, that it would not be possible for someone to act with intelligence and integrity, by simply trying to follow rules, no matter how well crafted or carefully qualified those rules may be. Someone who is attempting to follow rules must, at nearly every point, rely on good judgment, draw upon deeper principles, and view his action in relation to various idealizations. The ability to do this well is an ethical capacity. Thus, simply to follow rules well requires an appropriate ethical orientation.

Perhaps an analogy will help bring home this point. The Founding Fathers of the United States were clear that laws and government would not function well without a virtuous citizenry. A system of law, no matter how prudently devised, would work well only for a people who had good character, who understood the foundations of the law and who were prepared to live accordingly: "no free government, or the blessings of liberty, can be preserved to any people, but by a firm adherence to justice, moderation, temperance, frugality, and virtue, and by frequent recurrence to fundamental principles."[17]   In effect, they viewed good laws and a good constitution as a necessary but not a sufficient condition for a flourishing body politic. But the same holds true for any set of rules and any code, including codes of professional ethics.

Yet if this is so, what more is needed besides rules and a code? As we have already seen, what one needs additionally are *principles* and *good character*.

Principles. The term 'principle' is ambiguous. It can mean either (a) a high-level generalization or rule, or (b) a person's commitment to various goods, as having a certain priority, which is expressed in such a generalization or rule.

Call the former an 'external principle', because a principle in that sense is something apart from oneself, which one 'asserts' or 'formulates' or 'recognizes'. Examples of principles in that sense would be such rules as: "Avoid fraud and complicity in fraud above all", or "The public interest should be kept in view as the good that is served by public

---

[17] From the Declaration of Rights affixed to the Virginia Constitution of 1776.

accounting work." Generally, codes of ethics as articulated by professions or corporations consist of such 'external' principles.

But clearly 'external principles' suffer from many of the infirmities of rules. Moreover, because they are *formulations* or *expressions* of something else, external principles are derivative. If no one were 'principled' in some prior sense, no one would even be motivated to formulate a code of ethics, or have the requisite insight for formulating a good code.

The other sense of 'principle' is of an internal understanding of and commitment to the goods, and to the ordering of goods, expressed in an external principle. Whereas the rule, "Avoid fraud above all" is an external principle, a practitioner's *understanding* of this rule and of why it is important, together with his or her actual resolve and *commitment* never to commit a fraud, as shown in and tested by practice, would be an 'internal principle'. A person who has that kind of understanding and commitment 'has principles'. He or she *'works from, exemplifies*, or *embodies* a sound understanding of the basic principles of his field'. An internal principle, then, is a person's understanding of, and proven commitment to, an external principle.

External principle: a high-level generalization or rule.
Internal principle: a commitment to an ordering of goods.

Good character. We shall examine good character (and what have classically been referred to as the 'virtues') in the next chapter. What should be noted here is that, for someone to act well, it is not enough that he or she have a good knowledge or clear understanding of what he or she should do. Clearly someone could know or understand the right principle well enough, but not carry it out, or be disposed to carry it out, in practice. Nor, in fact, is it enough if someone simply has a commitment to the right principle and a strong resolve to carry it out. The reason is that frequently a person's inclinations, desires, and incentives can be at odds with his or her resolve. Thus, a practitioner also needs to be the sort of person who can easily, and without trouble, carry out what he or she has properly resolved. And this would be to have good character.

> Good character: traits of character that dispose us to carry out promptly and well what we judge to be right, and which protect against distortions of judgment.

A fairly clear example of the importance of good character generally for a practitioner has to do with *greed*. We may define greed as the desire or wish to have 'as much wealth as possible'. Greed therefore is of its nature unlimited; it is never truly satisfied. Greed is not, for instance, a desire for the exact capital needed for some specific enterprise; neither is it a desire for a sufficiency of wealth to raise a family with moderate advantages and ease. Both of these desires are limited, and when one reaches the stipulated amount, the desire vanishes. But greed, as is well recognized, is never satisfied. It sets goals for itself, but once these are met, it immediately is dissatisfied and looks for more.

> Greed: the wish or desire to acquire as much wealth as possible, not subject to constraints.

Now acting in a fair and principled way will always involve accruing wealth as subject to constraints. Indeed, typically to be fair means to accept *less* wealth than if one were not fair (as, for instance, when one returns money that one acquired through a mistaken overpayment). Thus, fairness and justice require that a person be regularly disposed to seek and accept wealth as conforming to certain limits. For this reason, greed and fairness are at odds with each other. A person who suffers from greed will be constantly tempted to act unfairly. These temptations would arise from his character—because, as hypothesized, this person is *greedy*—not from circumstances, and thus this motive will always potentially be influencing his thoughts and motives. In contrast, good character is contrary to greed and tends to correct or minimize it. So someone who had good character, in being less disposed to feel greed, would thereby be protected from this important influence, which threatens to shift someone from a good commitment and resolve.

Good character generally works in that way. It is a kind of safeguard and hedge against those non-rational motives that have the ability to sway us from our resolve to carry out the best course of action.

It should be clear that internal principles and good character remedy the deficiencies in rules that we noted above. For instance, consider point 1 above, that rules give only necessary but not sufficient conditions for proper action. Someone who understands and is committed to the correct principles will not rest content with having followed all the relevant rules. He will examine the particular circumstances he is in, and he will check to be sure that the goods he aims to promote are indeed safeguarded in these circumstances, and in the correct priority. Any temptations he might have to the contrary would not arise, because of his good character.

These considerations make it clear why an accountant needs to go deeper than principles, and that a study of ethics is important for an accountant. A good course in ethics should help the practitioner:

- Attain a thorough understanding of the goods aimed at by the profession of accounting and their correct ordering.
- Recognize the importance of good character, so that he or she takes direct and effective steps to acquire good character, to grow in good character, and to avoid actions or influences that might adversely affect his character.

That is to say, a good course in ethics should help a practitioner in just those areas in which rules are deficient. It should help him or her understand better the ethical principles underlying accountancy, and thereby to have a firmer commitment to those principles, and to those traits of character that would assist him or her in maintaining those principles.

Good rules are not enough, but neither are good principles, in the external sense. In a word: good rules and (external) principles must be interpreted and applied by a person who is himself or herself good. But that is what accounting ethics practically speaking aims at: How do we become in the relevant respects good professionals?

Two approaches to rules: Do they serve or trump principles?

Let us consider the relationship between rules and principles from another angle. As we have seen, rules do not exist on their own: rules are used by and are meant to guide a reasonable interpreter. But that means that the relationship between rules and principles is not fixed: it is something that we are free to alter, based on how we look upon rules. Basically, we are faced with a choice: we can either regard rules as expressing and safeguarding principles—call this "rules in the service of principles"—or take rules as sufficient and fully determinative of any relevant principles—call this "rules as trumping principles".

A common example in accounting illustrates the point, viz. whether for purposes of accounting a lease should be treated as an operating lease or a capital lease. As introductory accounting books will explain, leases fall along a scale: at one end of which is a pure rental arrangement, where some property is used for a short term in exchange for what amounts to rent; at the other end of which is a mortgage type arrangement, where ownership is effectively transferred from lessor to lessee, and the lease payments are in substance the same as payments on outstanding debt. Although there are close calls and difficult cases, there is typically a fact of the matter as to whether the lessee assumes the benefits and burdens of ownership, and thus the lease is of the latter type.

Now how would one deal with this issue of the proper treatment of a lease if taking the approach of "rules in the service of principles"? First, one would articulate the relevant principles and take these to be ultimately authoritative. For instance:

> Principle 1: The accounting treatment of a transaction should fairly represent that transaction. (The principle of transparency.)
> Principle 2: When the burdens and benefits of ownership are assumed by the lessee, then, although the transaction has the form of a lease, in substance it is equivalent to a mortgage arrangement. (The principle of 'substance over form'.)

Next, one might articulate rules which would serve as 'rules of thumb' for identifying when the condition mentioned in Principle 2 obtains, viz. when in fact what has the form of a lease is in substance the purchase of property with 100% financing. FASB 13 articulates four such rules, which we may summarize as follows (omitting some technicalities and qualifications):

> Rule 1. If ownership is transferred at the end of the lease, then the lease should be treated as a capital lease.

Rule 2. If the lessee has an option to buy the property at a bargain price (below market value), thus effectively guaranteeing purchase, then the lease should be treated as a capital lease.

Rule 3. If the length of the lease is for at least 75% of the total useful life of the property, then the lease should be treated as a capital lease.

Rule 4. If the lease payments equal at least 90% of the value of the property, then the lease should be treated as a capital lease.

We would be taking the approach of "rules in the service of principles" if we were to state clearly that the principles are paramount and authoritative in the interpretation of the rules. Thus: if following the rules were to result in an accounting treatment that represented as an operating lease a transaction in which, in fact, ownership is transferred, then the rules would have to give way to the principles. In actual practice, of course, what happens is that there is some latitude in how one estimates fair value and income stream, so that it can often happen that either an operating lease or a capital lease treatment could be reasonably defended, depending upon how one fixes the parameters. So the rules alone would give no determinate answer, and the practitioner would need to decide upon that accounting treatment that both accords with the rules and preserves the principles.

On the other hand, a practitioner would be taking the approach of "rules trumping principles" if the only question that he or she considered was whether the numbers could reasonably be manipulated to justify whatever accounting treatment was desired. (And in some cases an operating lease treatment may be more advantageous for a company's financial report than a capital lease treatment.) In that case, the practitioner would be approaching the accounting issue as if 'rules *were* enough'—when they clearly are not.

An example from GAAP

It is interesting that even relatively authoritative presentations of accounting principles can blur the distinction between rules as *serving* and rules as *trumping* principles. For instance, Miller's *Comprehensive*

GAAP Guide begins its discussion of the accounting· treatment of leases well enough:

> Some lease agreements are such that an asset and a related liability should be reported on the balance sheet of an enterprise. The distinction is one of substance over form (basic principle) when the transaction actually *transfers substantially all the benefits and risks inherent in the ownership of the property.*

When the *Guide* cites the maxim of 'substance over form', this is equivalent to saying that principles are prior to rules. So far so good. But then the *Guide* continues:

> Established in GAAP are criteria to determine whether a lease transaction is in substance a transfer of the incidents of ownership. If, at its inception, a lease meets one or more of the following four criteria, the lease should be classified as a transfer of ownership... [The four rules from FASB 13 are then given.]

But here the *Guide* lapses inadvertently into language that suggests that rules trump principles. Rules or criteria in fact do not *determine* (as the *Guide* puts it) whether a lease transaction is in substance a transfer of ownership. They do not determine this in the sense that they are not exhaustive (they are necessary but not sufficient conditions), and they may be indeterminate in their application and require good judgment: as we have seen, a transaction can frequently either satisfy one of the criteria or not do so, depending upon defensible judgments as to value and income. Thus to say, as the Miller Guide does, that these criteria 'determine' whether ownership is transferred is to invite and even encourage the view that the rules are enough and that the relevant principles can be put aside.

Some texts from classical philosophers

Some well-known classical texts are strikingly relevant to the points introduced above. Aristotle, in these texts from his major treatise on ethics, the *Nicomachean Ethics* (written around 340 B.C.), emphasizes the open-endedness of rules, and the need to use good judgment.

(Ethical rules are necessarily open-ended.)

"Our claims are adequate if they are made as clear as the subject matter allows. One shouldn't look for the same sort of accuracy in all subjects—just as practitioners in different crafts do not all aim to achieve the same sort of accuracy. But good practical judgment deals with admirable and equitable actions, which involve a great deal of variation and many exceptions. (Because of this, such actions are thought to be only conventionally admirable and equitable, not by nature so. But even good things have a certain unpredictability, because in many circumstances they result in harm—it's happened often enough that people have been ruined by wealth; and others have been ruined because they were courageous.) One should be satisfied, then, when one is proposing claims about these sorts of things, and starts from premises that have that sort of character, if one succeeds in stating the truth roughly and in outline. And when one is discussing matters that are 'for the most part' true, and starts from premises of that sort, one should be satisfied if one's conclusions are like that also. Moreover, someone should accept or reject the various things that we claim in the same fashion. It's a mark of being well-educated, that a person expect only that degree of accuracy that matches the kind of thing one is talking about—to seek as much accuracy, and only as much accuracy, as the nature of the thing allows. It seems to amount to much the same thing, to rest satisfied with rhetorical arguments from a mathematician, and to expect demonstrative arguments from a rhetorician" (1.3.1094b11-27).

(Rules require good judgment.)

"Every law is general, but as regards some matters it is not possible to speak in a general way with complete correctness. In those matters about which one needs to speak in a general way, but as regards which it is not possible to do so with complete correctness, the law is satisfied with speaking about what happens 'for the most part'—and when it does so, it is not ignorant of the fact that it is going astray.

"Yet, for all that, the law is correct. Why? Because the shortcoming is not in the law. It's not in the lawgiver, either. Rather, it is in the nature of the thing legislated about: the subject matter of actions is like this, from the very start.

"Thus: whenever the law would speak in a general way, but something not anticipated in the generalization takes place, for the reason mentioned, then everything will work out as it should if, in that respect in which the lawgiver was deficient and fell short because he failed to make the requisite qualification, one corrects the deficiency with *what the lawgiver would have set down as law if he were present and knew the situation.* That is why good judgment of that sort is equitable and is even better than one sort of justice: it's not better than justice itself, but it's better than justice which, because it is not suitably qualified, goes astray.

"And that is the nature of good judgment: it is a remedy for a deficiency in law, insofar as such deficiency is attributable to the general character that law must have. This is the reason as well that not everything falls under a law—because for some matters it is impossible to set down a law. It's necessary, then, as regards these things, to make particular rulings " (5.10.1137b13-29).

(Our commitment to principles is preserved by good character.)

"What pleases or displeases us does not corrupt or overturn just any working presupposition that we may have—for instance, whether or not a triangle is composed of two right angles—but rather those working presuppositions that involve action. Why? Because the principles of our actions involve that for the sake of which we do our actions. And when, because of pleasure or pain, this gets corrupted, then our principles become unclear; it also becomes unclear whether we should be aiming at and doing everything for the sake of that. Vice is in fact a corruption of our principles" (6.5.1140b13-20).

A relevant legal case

We have argued so far that ethics is indispensable for accounting practice. But, because of this, a practitioner who does not aim to act ethically, will not even succeed in acting legally. The cases in law that we consider in this book are cautionary examples of this truth.

A case that illustrates nicely that 'rules are not enough' is *U.S. v Simon*, 425 F.2d 796 (2nd Cir. 1969). Simon was a senior partner with Lybrand, Ross Bros. & Montgomery, who was convicted, along with fellow members of Lybrand, under the Securities Exchange Act of 1934, of drawing up and certifying a false and misleading financial statement, when auditing Continental Vending Machine Corporation ('Continental'). Continental's president was one Harold Roth, who had a 25% stake in both Continental and an affiliate company, Valley Commercial Corporation ('Valley'), and who essentially controlled both companies. Valley's business was ostensibly to provide financing for vending machine companies, including Continental. Eventually it became a money-laundering instrument for Roth. Roth would raid money from Continental in order to fund his speculations in the stock market. He did this by having Continental transfer money to Valley, in transactions that had no legitimate business purpose, and then personally 'borrowing' the money from Valley.

At first, these transfers of money from Continental to Valley (called by Roth the 'Valley Receivable') were small in comparison with the legitimate loans that Valley, in conjunction with various banks, extended to Continental (the 'Valley payable'). Moreover, Roth's investments did well enough, so that he was able to return the money to Valley, and transfer it back to Continental, by year's end. But when Roth's investments went south, and he became desperate and in need of larger sums, his raids on Continental became progressively larger, and his ability to return the money became more problematic, as the following table indicates:

Year	Advances to Valley	Repayments by Valley	Receivable at Year-End
1958	$3,356,239	$2,583,172	$0
1959	4,586,000	3,510,451	384,402
1960	2,511,000	2,670,500	397,996
1961	2,390,674	1,520,000	848,006
1962	4,708,000	1,986,500	3,543,335

By September of 1962, Roth informed Simon that Valley would fall short of repayment by the $3.5MM indicated on the table above. Roth's lawyer and Simon then contrived to secure approximately that amount with collateral provided by Roth. To indicate this, Simon composed the following footnote, which was included in the 1962 financial report which Simon drew up and certified:

2. The amount receivable from Valley Commercial Corp. (an affiliated company of which Mr. Harold Roth is an officer, director and stockholder) bears interest at 12% a year. Such amount, less the balance of the notes payable to that company, is secured by the assignment to the Company of Valley's equity in certain marketable securities. As of February 15, 1963, the amount of such equity at current market quotations exceeded the net amount receivable.

But there were various deficiencies in this footnote: it treated the 'Valley Receivable' as though it could be offset by the 'Valley Payable' (which it could not, because the latter was a legitimate loan owed to Valley along with several banks); it failed to indicate *that* Valley was simply unable to repay; and it failed to indicate *why* Valley was unable to repay. Furthermore, the collateral which Roth had offered consisted largely of shares from Continental itself (!), which clearly could have value only if Continental's financial condition was secure, which was precisely what was in doubt. Finally, the value of such collateral as Roth had offered had plummeted after the end of 1962, before the publication of the report, and this was known to Simon.

In its prosecution of the case, government attorneys and experts offered their own version of how footnote 2 should have been written, if it were not to be deceptive:

2. The amount receivable from Valley Commercial Corp. (an affiliated company of which Mr. Harold Roth is an officer, director and stockholder), which bears interest at 12% a year, was uncollectible at September 30, 1962, since Valley had loaned approximately the same amount to Mr. Roth who was unable to pay. Since that date Mr. Roth and others have pledged as security for the repayment of his obligation to Valley and its obligation to Continental (now $3,900,000, against which Continental's liability to Valley cannot be offset) securities which, as of February 15, 1963, had a market value of $2,978,000. Approximately 80% of such securities are stock and convertible debentures of the Company.

What is of interest for our purposes, is that Simon's attorneys were able to find many expert witnesses—experienced accountants—who testified that Simon's footnote 2 was entirely in accord with GAAP and GAAS! As the Court observes:

The defendants called eight expert independent accountants, an impressive array of leaders of the profession. They testified generally that, except for the error with respect to netting, the treatment of the Valley receivable in Note 2 was in no way inconsistent with generally accepted accounting principles or generally accepted auditing standards, since it made all the informative disclosures reasonably necessary for fair presentation of the financial position of Continental as of the close of the 1962 fiscal year. Specifically, they testified that neither generally accepted accounting principles nor generally accepted auditing standards required disclosure of the make-up of the collateral or of the increase of the receivable after the closing date of the balance sheet, although three of the eight stated that in light of hindsight they would have preferred that the make-up of the collateral be disclosed. The witnesses likewise testified that disclosure of the Roth borrowings from Valley was not required, and seven of the eight were of the opinion that such disclosure would be inappropriate. The principal reason given for this last view was that the balance sheet was concerned solely with presenting the financial position of the company under audit;

since the Valley receivable was adequately secured in the opinion of the auditors and was broken out and shown separately as a loan to an affiliate with the nature of the affiliation disclosed, this was all that the auditors were required to do. To go further and reveal what Valley had done with the money would be to put into the balance sheet things that did not properly belong there; moreover, it would create a precedent which would imply that it was the duty of an auditor to investigate each loan to an affiliate to determine whether the money had found its way into the pockets of an officer of the company under audit, an investigation that would ordinarily be unduly wasteful of time and money.

This expert testimony was rejected by the jury, which, as mentioned, found Simon and his associates guilty. The appeals court sustained the verdict, observing:

We join defendants' counsel in assuming that the mere fact that a company has made advances to an affiliate does not ordinarily impose a duty on an accountant to investigate what the affiliate has done with them or even to disclose that the affiliate has made a loan to a common officer if this has come to his attention. But it simply cannot be true that an accountant is under no duty to disclose what he knows when he has reason to believe that, to a material extent, a corporation is being operated not to carry out its business in the interest of all the stockholders but for the private benefit of its president. For a court to say that all this is immaterial as a matter of law if only such loans are thought to be collectible would be to say that independent accountants have no responsibility to reveal known dishonesty by a high corporate officer. If certification does not at least imply that the corporation has not been looted by insiders so far as the accountants know, or, if it has been, that the diversion has been made good beyond peradventure (or adequately reserved against) and effective steps taken to prevent a recurrence, it would mean nothing, and the reliance placed on it by the public would be a snare and a delusion. Generally accepted accounting principles instruct an accountant

what to do in the usual case where he has no reason to doubt
that the affairs of the corporation are being honestly conducted.
Once he has reason to believe that this basic assumption is false,
an entirely different situation confronts him.

Note the court's claim that what 'ordinarily' holds—that is, what gets
defined by rules—is not sufficient to determine what counts as correct
in this particular case. Rather, the court refers to the role of an
accountant in fostering public trust and the 'reliance' placed by the
investor or creditor on an audit report.

There are two ways to interpret the court's decision. One is to say
that Simon failed in fact to follow GAAP and GAAS, because accepted
accounting rules require that material facts be disclosed, and the nature
of Continental's advances to Valley was certainly material. But the court
takes a different approach. It concedes the claim of the defendant's that
their report and certification were in conformity with all definite rules
comprised by GAAP and GAAS under a defensible interpretation of
those rules, but it maintains that these rules require judgment in their
application, and that the ideals of disclosure and transparency, essential
to an accountant's role, must be decisive, when merely following rules
would yield a misleading result.[18]

That is to say: rules are not enough. And, for the jury which decided
Simon's guilt, this was basic commonsense.

---

[18] Compare *SEC v. Seaboard Corp.*, 677 F.2d 1301, 1313 n. 15 (9th Cir. 1989), n15: "We
have said that an accountant has no duty beyond compliance with generally accepted
accounting standards to ensure his client's honesty and to enforce his client's duty with
the security acts and regulations, see *SEC v. Arthur Young & Co.*, 590 F.2d 785, 788 (9th
Cir. 1979). But we have noted, with reference to *United States v. Simon*, 425 F.2d 796 (2nd
Cir. 1969), cert. denied 397 U.S. 1006, 90 S. Ct. 1235, 25 L. Ed. 2d 420 (1970), that in
certain circumstances generally accepted accounting principles will not immunize an
accountant if he consciously chose not to disclose a known material fact."

Chapter 2 Review
Learning Objectives and Review Questions

Learning Objectives

After reading this chapter you should be able to:
• Distinguish necessary from sufficient conditions.
• Identify appeals to ideal standards in rules.
• Illustrate the use of good judgment in the application of rules.
• Explain the dependence of rules upon principles.

Questions for Review

1. It is a necessary condition of there being puddles on the ground that it had previously rained. True or false?
2. It is a sufficient condition of there being puddles on the ground that it had previously rained. True or false?
3. Rules of accounting practice give conditions that suffice for propriety. True or false?
4. Which of the following rules refer to cases that could not in principle be explicitly enumerated?
    a. "No species of beetle is endothermic."
    b. "Independence is affected if a close relative is an executive of the firm."
    c. "Every review is distinct from an audit."
    d. "Independence is to be sought for in an accountant."
5. Consider the rule: "A member should refuse an engagement with an enterprise if his or her spouse does audit-sensitive work for the enterprise." Which of the following adds nothing to this?
    a. "It's an important rule that a member should refuse an engagement with an enterprise if his spouse does audit-sensitive work for the enterprise."
    b. "Always obey the rule that a member should refuse an engagement with an enterprise if his or her spouse does audit-sensitive work for the enterprise."

c. "A member should refuse an engagement with an enterprise if his or her spouse does audit-sensitive work for the enterprise.— Or that's what I agreed to, when I agreed to join the profession of public accountants."

d. "A member will appear to lack independence if he or she does not refuse an engagement with an enterprise, when his or her spouse does audit-sensitive work for the enterprise."

e. a. and b.

f. c. and b.

6. Which of the following is not an example of proportionate or due diligence?

a. Assessing the risk of fraud when carrying out an audit.

b. Withdrawing from an engagement when a conflict of interest develops.

c. Treating even the slightest intentional misrepresentation by an executive as material.

d. Giving the benefit of the doubt to reported figures in a review.

7. Ignorance of ethical principles can sometimes excuse a bad action. True or false?

8. Which of the following is an internal principle?

a. ET Section 54, Article III—Integrity.

b. A member's incorrect understanding of ET Section 54, Article III.

c. A particular interpretation rendered by the relevant rule-making body of the AICPA.

d. SAS 99.

9. Complete the following sentence from Aristotle. "And when one is talking about matters that are _____ true and beginning with premises of that sort, it's enough if our conclusions are like that also."

a. always.

b. sometimes.

c. never.

d. for the most part.

10. Complete the following sentence from Aristotle. "Thus: whenever the law would speak in a general way, but something not comprehended

in the generalization takes place, for the reason mentioned, then everything works out as it should if, in that respect in which the law giver was deficient and fell short because he failed to make a qualification, one corrects the deficiency with _____."

    a. one's best guess at what is right.

    b. what reason and tradition imply is right.

    c. what the lawgiver would have said if he were present and knew the facts.

    d. what similar laws in other societies say.

11. *U.S. v. Simon* in some respects bears an uncanny resemblance to:

    a. The Enron scandal.

    b. The Tyco scandal.

    c. The WorldCom scandal.

    d. None of the above.

Suggested Answers

1. False. It's possible that there be puddles from, for example, someone's washing his car outside earlier in the day.

2. False. On a very hot day, or if the rain shower is brief, it can rain without leaving puddles.

3. False. In many circumstances it is possible to follow the rules but violate the substance of what the rules were meant to insure.

4. b. Many different circumstances, accidental and unforeseeable in advance, could make it turn out that someone who would not ordinarily be counted as a 'close' relative would in fact be 'close', or that a relationship is the equivalent of that. But (for (a)) there are a finite number of species of beetle, which could in principle all be examined. And (for (b)) the distinction between a review and an audit is definitional. And (d) refers to a single ideal.

5. e. What is at issue here is whether a statement goes beyond simply asserting another rule. But (c) appeals to a commitment more basic than rules; and (d) extends the rule to include the appearance of impropriety, thereby in fact bringing in the relevant principle or ideal.

6. b. This is an example of lack of independence. The other alternatives imply a responsibility to discover or investigate in order to acquire more information.

7. False. Ignorance of the relevant general principles is always culpable.

8. b. An internal principle is something understood by a practitioner, which motivates the practitioner, as thus understanding it. It is a characteristic of a person. The other alternatives all involve statements and assertions, which are external to us.

9. d. Rules for practical matters are true only for the most part ('generally', 'typically', 'in ordinary circumstances', 'standardly').

10. c. The importance of the appeal to what the lawgiver would say is that it draws our attention to the ideals and principles which, necessarily, were prior to the lawgiver's public articulation of a law.

11. b. In the Tyco scandal similarly management was alleged to have raided company funds for private purposes, without interference from outside auditors who either did know or should have known of the impropriety.

3

Elements of Ethics

THE STUDY OF ACCOUNTING ETHICS is the application, to the profession of accounting, of basic principles of ethics. Therefore, the study of accounting ethics presupposes some study of ethics in general. Our task in this chapter, then, is to become acquainted with some basic notions and principles of ethics in general. In the next chapter, we examine the AICPA Code of Professional Conduct in light of these notions and principles. And, as mentioned, in the final two chapters we apply these notions and principles to case studies of accounting fraud in Enron and WorldCom.

Ethical reasoning versus a theory of ethics

All of us are constantly engaged, in everything that we do, whether we like it or not, whether we deliberately wish to do so or not, in ethical reasoning and judgment. We reason ethically when we wonder and consider whether something or some course of action is *good* or *bad*; *appropriate* or *inappropriate*; *fair* or *unfair*; *right* or *wrong*. Jones is driving to work and someone cuts her off, violating her right of way—"That's unfair!", she thinks about what was done to her. "What a jerk!", she says to herself, making a judgment about that other person's character. What the example illustrates is that even when she is simply driving to work,

Jones presupposes ethical principles involving how we should drive and treat one another. Something as mundane as driving to work is not 'ethically neutral'.

When she arrives at work, she immediately gets down to business, not wasting time—a point of 'honor' for her (which is an ethical notion)—and she keeps her appointments and gets to them on time, which is a matter of *fairness* and *justice* in her relationships with others. In the work itself that she does as well, ethical considerations are always present: Has she offered a fair amount of work in return for the payment she is receiving? Were the statements she made truthful? Did she conceal or gloss over shoddy or incomplete work?

And then how Jones in general balances her commitment to professional work with the time and affection she owes her husband and family, and the time she recognizes that she should spend in service to her community, also involve judgments that are ethical in character. And all of this is so far not even to touch upon her interior thoughts, inclinations, and affections—which are present with her throughout the day and determine the motive of what she does and its true worth.

> Ethical action is something we all engage in, unavoidably so. It is an inescapable part of the human condition.

But at times we find that we need to get clearer about ethical reasoning and action. Perhaps a dilemma presents itself, and we need to articulate a principle that would resolve it. (For instance, should Jones decline an invitation for dinner with a client in order to attend her daughter's soccer game?) Or perhaps a disaster involving a friend or colleague—someone's professional failure or disgrace; personal problems; an inadequate response to a personal tragedy—makes us wonder whether we are living as we should. And sometimes we simply want to understand better the basic principles on which we act, because this is worthwhile in itself, or because we sense that this will make us a better professional. In every such case we somehow need to go more deeply than ordinary, commonsense ethical reasoning.

In view of this, a distinction is sometimes drawn between ethical reasoning, and a theory of ethical reasoning. A theory of ethical reasoning is meant to be systematic thought, which renders more explicit the patterns and principles of reasoning that are implicit in ordinary ethical reasoning. Once such principles are made explicit, then, it is thought, we can examine them, understand them better, refine them and systematize them.

Such a considered and more systematic outlook may be called a 'theory' of ethical reasoning.

> A theory of ethics: systematic thought, which renders more explicit the patterns and principles of reasoning that are implicit in ordinary ethical reasoning.

Grammar provides something of an analogy. When we speak English, we implicitly regard some ways of speaking as appropriate and others not. Most of the time, we take these things for granted and do not deliberate about them. But some people (professional grammarians), aim to make these considerations explicit, and then that sort of explicit reflection on grammar can undeniably help us to write and speak more effectively and clearly. Philosophers, in thinking systematically about ethics, take on the role of 'grammarians' of ethical reasoning; a good theory of ethics can help us act better, much as grammar can help us speak and write better.

Types of ethical theory

Nearly everything in philosophy is up for debate, and, naturally enough, different philosophers have proposed different and incompatible systematizations of ethical reasoning. Perhaps the three most important of these are: (i) consequentialism (or 'utilitarianism') ; (ii) Kantianism; and (iii) classical or 'virtue' ethics. In this book, we adopt classical or 'virtue' ethics as our framework of ethical deliberation. But we should briefly explain why we do not accept the other theories.

> The three principal ethical theories are: consequentialism, Kantianism, and classical or 'virtue' ethics.

(i) Consequentialism is the view that *the rightness or wrongness of an action depends solely on the consequences of an action for people's welfare in general.* Consequentialism holds that an action is right and should be done if it is that action, of all those actions available to us, which leads to the greatest surplus of good over bad, for people considered generally. Basically, it holds that we should act in such a way as to maximize the good consequences of our actions. Historically, the most important version of consequentialism has been utilitarianism; and the most important proponent of utilitarianism was the 19th c. English philosopher, John Stuart Mill.

> Consequentialism: the rightness or wrongness of an action depends solely on the consequences of an action for people's welfare.

We reject consequentialism as a satisfactory theory of ethics, for three reasons:

1. Some actions which are possibly right, according to consequentialism, in fact are always clearly wrong. For instance, slavery is possibly right according to consequentialism: in particular, slavery would be right, when enslaving some persons would be best for society in general. But clearly slavery can never be right. The wrongness of slavery serves, then, as a counterexample to consequentialism.

2. Consequentialism is a departure from, and is not an accurate systematization of, ordinary ethical reasoning. Most ethical reasoning involves recognizing actions as inherently appropriate, fitting, and fair, and therefore to be done, or as the opposite of these, and therefore to be avoided. Consequentialism takes one aspect of ordinary ethical reasoning—namely, 'instrumental rationality', or means-end reasoning with a view to efficiency—and makes this equivalent to the whole.

3. The most important action that we engage in is thinking. However, thinking is not governed by consequentialist considerations. For instance, one of the best examples of thinking is mathematical deduction and proof. At each step of a proof, the step that we *ought* to take is that which is *rationally required*, not the step that leads to the best consequences (which in fact we pay no heed to, when doing the proof).

Accurate and truthful thinking in general is similarly not carried out with a view to consequences. But if consequentialism cannot account well for the most important sort of action we engage in, then it fails as a theory of human ethical action.

> Consequentialism is to be rejected, since:
> It says that some wrong actions can sometimes be right.
> It construes ethical reasoning as merely means-end reasoning.
> It cannot account for the worth of the most important human activities.

(ii) Kantianism. Kantianism is the theory of ethics formulated by the late 18th century German philosopher Immanuel Kant. Kant regarded ethics as a system of law governing the relations among ideally rational, free, and autonomous persons. The most fundamental principle of ethics, according to Kant, is the 'Categorical Imperative': *always act in such a way that you could will that the maxim inherent in your action should serve as a law that binds rational agents generally.* For someone to reason ethically, Kant believed, was simply for him or her to apply the Categorical Imperative.

> The Categorical Imperative (Immanuel Kant):
> Always act in such a way that you could will that the maxim inherent in your action could serve as a law that binds rational agents generally.

But we also reject Kantianism as a satisfactory theory of ethics. There are various well-known difficulties with Kantianism. But we reject it principally for the following reasons.

1. Kantianism is unworkably abstract. The Categorical Imperative seems too abstract to resolve any particular moral question: in order to apply it, one needs to supplement it with other, substantive ethical principles. For instance, suppose someone commits suicide out of despair. Is suicide ruled out the by the Categorical Imperative? The maxim inherent in such an act of suicide would presumably be: "Kill

yourself when your future is bleak." But why *couldn't* someone will that this maxim be adopted by everyone, as a rule of action? In fact, this is just the general principle that members of the Hemlock Society endorse. So the Categorical Imperative is not sufficient to give guidance even in this relatively straightforward ethical question.

2. Kantianism is uninformative because it is formalistic. Kantianism is a variant of what is called 'formalism' in ethics. As a formalist theory, it avoids, and gives no answer to, the 'substantive' question of who counts as a 'rational agent' and therefore falls under the scope of the Categorical Imperative. For instance, a Nazi, who held that Jewish persons were 'subhuman', might have followed the Categorical Imperative perfectly in how he treated his German peers, while nonetheless exterminating the Jews. Similarly, Kantianism could have given no definite answer to the question of whether it was right to hold slaves. Clearly, if slaves are rational, autonomous agents, then Kantianism would hold that they cannot rightly be enslaved. But Kantianism itself gives no answer as to whether all human beings are rational and autonomous agents. (For similar reasons, Kantianism is incapable today of deciding the issue of abortion.)

3. Kantianism is unrealistically impartial. Kantianism holds that the mark of ethical reasoning is universalizability: to be moral is to examine one's own action by asking, "What if everyone did that?" But the great bulk of a person's ethical reasoning will involve one's spouse, children, or friends; and these are *particular* relationships, which we have with some persons only and not others. In these cases it is hardly helpful to ask, "What if everyone did that?"—because no one else is related to those persons in the same way. In short, if it were workable at all, Kantianism could give direction only as to how to treat strangers, or how to deal with others with complete impartiality: it could not give good direction about how to treat family members or close friends.

> Kantianism is objectionable because it is: unworkably abstract; impractically formalistic; and unrealistically impartial.

(iii) 'Classical' ethical theory is sometimes also called 'virtue ethics' or 'virtue theory'. It considers what good traits of character a person should have, in order to be a good human being. It studies and classifies these traits, and then it regards an action as good or bad, depending upon whether it is the sort of action that would be done by someone having those good traits.

In classical ethical theory, four good traits of character have been identified as the most fundamental:

Courage ('bravery' or 'fortitude')
Moderation ('self-mastery' or 'temperance')
Justice ('fairness' or 'uprightness')
Prudence ('good judgment' or 'good sense')

These four good traits are classically known as the 'cardinal' virtues.

> The term 'cardinal' comes from the Latin, *cardo*, which means a 'hinge'. These virtues are called 'cardinal' or 'hinge-like' on the grounds that all other good traits depend upon them.

On classical ethical theory, we decide whether an action is good or bad by first placing it in the proper domain, and then considering whether that action is the sort of thing that would be done by someone who had the virtue relevant to that domain. For instance, you are hiking in the Grand Canyon with a friend, who asks that you walk out onto a rock overhang, so that he can take a stunning picture of you with the Canyon as a backdrop. Should you walk out onto the overhang? Your initial state is one of fear and reluctance. But you are conflicted. On the one hand, you recognize that fear is often irrational, and that people should not hold back from doing something worthwhile because of irrational fear. On the other hand, you don't want to be reckless and endanger your life for a triviality. To go out on the overhang would involve danger, and the virtue relevant to acting well in circumstances of danger is courage. Classical ethics would suggest that walking out on the overhang to get your picture taken is what you should do, if it is the sort of thing that a courageous person would do in those circumstances.

(Should you do it, then? It depends on *how dangerous* it really would be to go out on that overhang.)

We regard the classical approach to ethics as particularly well suited to serving as a framework for the examination of accounting ethics, not simply because of its commonsense character and eminent practicality, but also because standards of professional conduct for accounting themselves appeal to 'virtues', and they encourage practitioners to look to the relevant virtue as a standard of correct action. For example, as we shall see more clearly in the next chapter, objectivity is a virtue in an accountant, and typically one can determine whether a course of action is correct by considering whether that is the sort of thing that would be done by someone who was suitably objective. It is evident that this is the manner of reasoning adopted on the classical theory.

Goodness and virtue

Virtue ethics holds that a virtue enables someone to carry out his task well. A virtue makes someone *good* as a performer of that task. We should pause for a moment, then, and give some attention to what goodness is.

It is a common view today that goodness is either (a) unreal or (b) subjective. But these views need to be rejected in order to understand accounting ethics, because it is fundamental to accounting ethics, as we construe it, that there is such a thing as being a good practitioner and a good professional, and whether a practitioner succeeds in exemplifying the ideals of the profession depends upon his or her truly being in the relevant respects good.

(a) The view that goodness is *unreal* is the view that, in effect, 'goodness is in the eye of the beholder'. On this view, goodness is something we fictitiously ascribe to things, or 'project' onto things, like the figures that we see in clouds, or the face that we discern in the Moon. The Moon does not really have a face, of course, but we ascribe or 'project' the appearance of a face onto the Moon. On this view, similarly, when we regard something as good, that thing in reality has no feature which makes it so: we are simply 'projecting' a positive quality onto it. Goodness is a bias or preference that we impute to things, but which does not really exist in things. Goodness is in the eye of the beholder.

But this view is not sustainable, for a variety of reasons. We shall mention two. The first reason is that this view renders ethical discussion, argument, and disagreement impossible. If I say that a cloud is a horse, and you say that it is a flower, we are not disagreeing, because neither of us is making a claim about how the cloud actually is; we are only expressing what we fictitiously imagine the cloud to be. If ethical discourse were like that, then no one could ever in fact *disagree* in ethics.

The second reason is that, even if we accepted this view, we would still have to acknowledge that there was something that was truly good and not a matter of a mere 'projection'. To see that this is so, suppose that to call something 'good' was to project a positive quality onto something. Yet some people would do this correctly and well, and others not. For instance, those people who project a *positive* quality onto world peace and a *negative* quality onto the Holocaust would do this well; whereas people who projected a *negative* quality onto world peace and a *positive* quality onto the Holocaust would not do this well. We would want to say that people who did this well would be, to that extent, *good*; and those who did not do this well would be, to that extent, *not good*. But this judgment in turn—whether these people are good or not— would not be a mere projection of a positive value, on pain of an infinite regress. So not all goodness can be unreal.

(b) The view that goodness is *subjective* is the view that, whenever someone calls something 'good', he is remarking on some relation that that thing has to him. 'Good' on this view might mean, for instance, 'useful *to me*', or 'attractive *to me*'. On this view, the term 'good' never refers to something that is the same for everyone.

But this view is also not sustainable. Suppose that to call something 'good' is to mean that it is 'useful for me'. Thus, when Jones says that something is good, what she means is that it is *useful for Jones.* However, Jones could be right about this, or wrong, and anyone in principle could recognize that she was right or wrong. And it would be *good* for her to be right, and *bad* for her to be wrong, and (likewise) anyone could recognize that this were so. Thus when Jones *rightly* claims that something is good, i.e. useful for her, it is good that she do so, and anyone could recognize this. But *this* goodness—the goodness of the truth of his assertion—as we saw, is not relative to her. Thus not all goodness is subjective.

If all goodness were subjective, then it would be *true* that all goodness were subjective. Thus it would be *good* for someone to say, "All goodness is subjective". But the goodness of the truth of this assertion would not *itself* be subjective.

We therefore reject the common view that goodness is unreal or subjective. We regard it as crucial to a sound approach to accounting ethics that these views be rejected.

The classical theory of ethics, in contrast, regards goodness as real, objective, and even something familiar and ordinary. Goodness is defined in the following way:

> **Goodness.** A thing of a certain kind is good, if it has those traits (or 'virtues') that enable it to carry out its distinctive work (or task) well.

For instance, the distinctive work or task of a knife is to cut. The traits that enable a knife to cut well include: having a sharp edge; holding a sharp edge; and having a safe, slip-resistant handle. A knife that had all of these features would be able to carry out its distinctive work well. Thus, a knife that had all of these features would be *good*, really and not subjectively.

Again, the distinctive work or task of a piano is to play keyboard music. The traits that enable a piano to play keyboard music well include: being in tune; staying in tune; having a rich tone; and having firm but responsive key action. A piano that had these traits would similarly be a good piano.

Thus, goodness on the classical theory is not something strange, mystical, subjective, or unreal. To be good is simply to be equipped with traits that enable a thing to do what it was designed or intended to do.

But how do we recognize the 'distinctive work' of a thing? The distinctive work of a thing is typically what that alone can do, or what that alone can do well. For instance, you are looking in a tool box, and you see a hammer, pliers, and a Phillips screwdriver. The screwdriver cannot bend wire; the hammer cannot turn screws; and the pliers cannot drive nails. The hammer alone can drive nails. The pliers alone, of all the tools in the toolbox, can bend wire. The Phillips tip screwdriver alone can turn a Phillips head screw. These tasks are then the 'distinctive work' of the corresponding kind of thing.

> The characteristic (or distinctive) work of a certain kind of thing is what that kind of thing alone can do, or do well.

On the classical theory of ethics, human virtues are those traits that enable a human being to carry out his characteristic work well. And what is the distinctive work of a human being? It is what a human being alone can do, or can do well. This is to act intelligently, and with a true promotion of the good of others, in the various domains of human social life. The traits that enable us to do this well are the virtues. And a person is good (really and truly) if he has those traits.

For instance, in human social life we often encounter circumstances of danger, in response to which we feel fear. The trait of character that enables us to act appropriately, even in the presence of something fearful, is *courage*. Again, in human social life, we often need to exchange, assign, or apportion goods of the sort that, generally, it would be desirable to have more of. The trait of character that enables someone to do so with a view to fairness and equality, not taking more than one should for oneself, is *justice*. Again, human beings are rational *animals*: we have an animal aspect to ourselves, then, which looks for ever more bodily pleasure, satisfaction, and comfort. The trait of character which enables us not to be deflected from doing what we should, and what is appropriate, because of a desire for bodily pleasures and comforts, is 'moderation' (or 'self-mastery').

Principles and character

If a thing has different parts, then it will typically have different virtues corresponding to those parts. Consider for instance a wine-bottle opener of the sort used by sommeliers in restaurants, consisting of a small knife (for cutting the wrapper), a corkscrew (for grabbing the cork), and a metal lever (for prying the cork out of the bottle). That sort of tool has three parts, and therefore it will have three different sorts of virtue. Its knife part should be sharp; its corkscrew part should have a pointed tip and be sturdy; its lever part should be the right shape and size and made out of sturdy metal.

> *Courage* is that trait which enables a person to act appropriately, that is, reasonably, in the presence of something fearful.
> *Justice* is that trait which enables a person to act appropriately, that is, to select what is fair and equal, in exchanges or distributions of commutable goods.
> *Moderation* is that trait which enables a person to act appropriately as regards bodily pleasures and comforts.

A human being also has different 'parts' that are relevant to carrying out one's distinctive task of acting intelligently and from a true promotion of the good of others. Generally, to act well we need (i) to think (or judge) correctly, and then we need (ii) to carry out well what we think we should do. For instance, to act well on the field of battle, we need to make good judgments about the threat posed by the enemy, and about the proper way of responding to that threat. Any judgment of that sort will imply feelings of fear (to judge that something is a threat will naturally inspire fear in the person making that judgment). And then we need to succeed in doing what we should do, given those feelings of fear.

Those traits that enable someone *to think correctly* about how he should act are classically referred to as 'intellectual virtues'. Those traits that enable someone *to carry out well* what he thinks he should do are classically referred to as 'virtues of character.'

Generally, to carry out well what one thinks one should do implies doing the right thing *promptly*; *resolutely* and *without divided motives*; *with* (some degree of) *pleasure*; and *without* any *distress* or regret because one is not doing something else. (We typically carry out something well only if we take pleasure in doing it.) For instance, someone who has courage will do what he thinks he should do on the field of battle immediately. He will do so without vacillation or second-thoughts. He will be pleased with himself for doing what he thinks he should do. And he will not be filled with regret or dissatisfaction because he did not choose a safe or cowardly course of action. Again, someone who has the virtue of justice actually *enjoys* seeing that everyone involved in a distribution or exchange gets treated fairly, even if a fair distribution implies that he gets significantly less.

Intellectual virtue: a trait that enables us to think correctly about what we should do.
Virtue of character: a trait that enables us, once we have decided what we should do, to carry out that action promptly, resolutely, with enjoyment, and without distress.

We pointed out in the last chapter that 'rules are not enough' and that a practitioner additionally needs good judgment. Good judgment is an intellectual virtue, which involves making use of sound principles, and appealing to ideal notions, such as what a 'reasonable' person would say. Yet now it is clear that even good judgment is not enough, because, in order to act well, one needs to be the sort of person who effectively carries out what good judgment says should be done, and, in order to do this, one needs good character.

The intellectual virtues include:
- Good judgment
- Being a good judge of character
- Discernment
- Understanding
- Perspective
- Balance
- Impartiality
- Objectivity
- Sagacity
- Administrative skill
- Knowledge

Virtues of character include:
- Courage

- Moderation
- Justice
- Generosity
- Easy-goingness
- Amiability
- Sense of honor
- Sense of integrity
- Love of truth
- Sincerity

One important difference between intellectual virtues and virtues of character, is that, whereas the former are acquired largely by study and instruction—by studying a book such as this, for instance—the latter are acquired only by practice. A virtue of character is acquired only by doing actions of the sort that are typical of that virtue. To become generous, a person needs actually to do generous-type actions. To develop a sense of integrity, a person needs actually to do actions of the sort that show integrity. Typically, we acquire a virtue of character by doing the relevant sorts of actions in some restricted or less significant field of action. A child, for instance, develops honesty by being truthful about relatively small and insignificant matters. A recruit grows in courage by field exercises which are successively closer in character to actual battle conditions. Because typically we acquire traits of character in relatively minor situations, indirectly related to those circumstances in which it is most important to exercise those traits, it happens that scrupulously good behavior in minor details ends up being very important for the development and maintenance of virtues of character.

In relation to this, consider a fear faced by nearly every external audit practitioner: that of losing a significant client. In an economic environment where bringing in new clients is usually rewarded and losing clients is punished, it is understandable why even someone imbued with all of the *intellectual virtues* would not fare well without the *virtues of character*. Consider a practitioner who is facing the economic pressures of a recent divorce, two children in college, a construction development facing cash calls, and a sick parent. The idea of losing one's relatively high paying job over pushing a client to accept an operating versus capital lease treatment in a circumstance where the client has "dotted the I's and crossed the T's" from a rules perspective seems unrealistic. This can be made all the more difficult in a circumstance where one's firm, and its senior partners, have supported such treatment in the past. And yet that may be exactly what is demanded of a practitioner, when considering that his primary duty is to the public trust, the company's stakeholders, and its long-term success. Those *virtues of character* of courage, love of truth, sense of integrity, and justice may demand that a big client's retention be put at risk. Consider how much easier this process might have been if the firm, and/or profession had been consistent on such matters in the past. Consider how much easier it might have been if that same practitioner had been consistently active in explaining to the clients that "substance over form" and "conservativism" are important, and they had seen him practice those principles in the past.

The answer to the question, Can ethics be taught?, and the key to restoring the reputation of the profession, are the same: this is to be found within the distinction between *intellectual virtues* that have to be *learned*, and *virtues of character* that have to be *practiced*.

Common good and law

We have looked briefly at what goodness in general is, and what goodness in a human being amounts to. Now we need to look briefly at some other basic notions of ethics, which serve as background to our specific treatment of accounting ethics in the next chapter.

For instance, the notion of 'public interest', so crucial to accounting ethics, is a particular application of the notion of 'common good'. Thus, it is useful to look briefly at the classical notion of 'common good'. But in order to get clear about the notion of a 'common good', it is necessary first to get clear about the notion of an *association*.

Very few things can be accomplished by a person on his own. Most of us do not grow our own food; haul water to our house; walk to work; or use home remedies to treat illnesses we have. Nearly all of the goods that we enjoy or procure are attained through cooperating with others. Sometimes this cooperation is direct, as when a worker carpools to drive to work. But usually it is indirect, through the marketplace, when one person pays another with money for a good or service, this money itself serving as a token of some good or service that he had earlier provided for someone else.

People form an association in order to procure some good, or enjoy a service, or achieve a result, that each could not attain at all, or attain easily, on his own.

> The purpose of any association is to procure some good or service, or to achieve a result, that each could not attain at all, or attain easily, on his own.

Every association involves reciprocity. Each member gives up trying to achieve some good on his own; he consents to receive it through the association; and therefore he directs his efforts at some coordinated plan of action required by the association.

For instance, consider farmers living on the coast of Ireland during the 9th century, who would regularly be attacked by Viking ships. Each farmer wants to defend his own family; but no farmer can do this successfully working on his own. Hence they form a militia, which is an association for common defense. When a farmer joins the militia, he gives up trying to defend his own homestead on his own, and he consents to serve whenever and wherever the commander of the militia requires. It might by accident happen that the commander assigns some farmer to guard a plot of land which is identical to that farmer's homestead. And in that case the farmer would, to all external appearances, be acting very much as if he were attempting to guard his homestead on his own. But in fact, in the case we are supposing, he would be acting, rather, to carry out the orders of the commander, as part of a coordinated plan of action.

Every association involves reciprocity. Someone gives up something to belong to it, in order to get something more valuable in return. In the example we have described, the reciprocity of the association consists in this: each member farmer gives up trying to defend his own homestead, and he receives in return the defense that the militia provides. That his homestead gets defended is a consequence or result of the militia doing its work of defending all of the farms. Prior to joining the militia, a farmer had as his good a *private* good only: the protection of his own homestead. After he joins the militia, a farmer has as his good a 'common good': his aim is to defend the various homesteads all together, according to the best plan of defense devised by the commander. This aim is shared by all of the farmers. Each aims to advance the efforts of the militia, for the 'common defense'. Moreover, each farmer understands that his private good now gets achieved as a *consequence* of the common good: it is through the common defense that his own homestead gets protected.

Each association, then, has a common good. It is something that all of the members of that association aim at, which implies as a consequence the achievement of the private good of each member. For instance, the common good of a baseball team would be winning games. The common good of a militia is the common defense. The common good of a carpool is getting to work efficiently.

> Common good: the goal aimed at by all of the members of an association, which is such that, when it is attained, each member of the association receives that good which was the reason why the association was formed in the first place.

Note that every common good implies a coordinated plan of action. The baseball team aims to win games by each person playing his position well. The militia aims at the common defense, by each farmer following the orders of a commander appointed for that purpose. This coordinated plan of action is the 'law' of that association. Each association requires coordinated action, and the rules that establish and effect that coordination are the law of that association. In society, associations form hierarchies, with larger associations having more authority than those that are subsumed under them. The largest association is simply political society itself. The law of this association in particular has the greatest authority and is typically referred to as 'law' simply.

> Law: a statement of the plan by which members of an association are to coordinate their action to achieve the common good of that association.

It is important to grasp that law is based on a conception of the common good, because the sound interpretation of a law will require that it be placed in relationship to the common good. [19]

Some classic texts

Here as in the first chapter we include some texts from classical authors which illustrate some of the principles that we have introduced and discussed.

(The characteristic work and distinctive virtue of a thing.)

"I will proceed by asking a question: Would you not say that a horse has some characteristic work? —I should.—And the characteristic work or use of a horse or of anything would be that which could not be accomplished, or not so well accomplished, by any other thing? —I do not understand, he said. —Let me explain: Can you see, except with the eye? —Certainly not. — Or hear, except with the ear? —No. —These then may be truly said to be the characteristic work of these organs? —They may. —But you can cut off a vine-branch with a dagger or with a chisel, and in many other ways? —Of course. —And yet not so well as with a pruning-hook made for the purpose? —True. — May we not say that this is the characteristic work of a pruning-hook? —We may. —Then now I think you will have no difficulty in understanding my meaning when I asked the question whether the characteristic work of anything would be that which could not be accomplished, or not so well accomplished, by any other thing? —I understand your meaning, he said, and assent. – –And that to which the characteristic work of a thing belongs has also a virtue? Need I ask again whether the eye has its

---

[19] With respect to the accounting profession there exist many associations to which a practitioner, whether internal or external, pledges or is necessitated to show allegiance. These can range from the AICPA, state CPA licensing boards, PCAOB, SEC, FASB, firm, company, and so on.

characteristic work? —It has. —And has not the eye a virtue? — Yes. —And the ear has its characteristic work and a virtue also? – –True. —And the same is true of all other things; they have each of them have their characteristic work and a special virtue? — That is so. —Well, and can the eyes carry out their characteristic work if they are wanting in their distinctive virtue and have a defect instead? —How can they, he said, if they are blind and cannot see? —You mean to say, if they have lost their distinctive virtue, which is sight. But I have not arrived at that point yet. I would rather ask the question more generally, and only enquire whether the things which carry out their characteristic work do so by their own distinctive virtue, and fail to carry them out by their own defect? —Certainly, he replied." (Plato, *Republic*, book I)

(Intellectual virtue and virtue of character.)

"Virtue, then, being of two kinds, intellectual and moral, intellectual virtue in the main owes both its birth and its growth to teaching (for which reason it requires experience and time), while moral virtue comes about as a result of habit, whence also its name (*êthike*) is one that is formed by a slight variation from the word *êthos* (habit)." (Aristotle, *Nicomachean Ethics*, 2.1)

(Virtue of character is acquired by doing similar actions.)

"It is from the same causes and by the same means that every virtue is both produced and destroyed, and similarly every art; for it is from playing the lyre that both good and bad lyre-players are produced. And the corresponding statement is true of builders and of all the rest; men will be good or bad builders as a result of building well or badly. For if this were not so, there would have been no need of a teacher, but all men would have been born good or bad at their craft. This, then, is the case with the virtues also; by doing the acts that we do in our transactions with other men we become just or unjust, and by doing the acts that we do in the presence of danger, and being habituated to feel fear or confidence, we become brave or cowardly. The same is true of appetites and feelings of anger; some men become temperate and good-tempered, others self-indulgent and irascible, by behaving in one way or the other in the appropriate circumstances. Thus, in one word, states of character arise out of like activities. This is why the activities we exhibit must be of a certain kind; it is because the states of character correspond to the differences between these. It makes no small difference, then, whether we form habits of one kind or of another from our very youth; it makes a very great difference, or rather all the difference" (Aristotle, *Nicomachean Ethics*, 2.1).

A relevant legal case

Although there are no legal cases involving accounting malfeasance that bear directly upon basics in ethical theory, a case that is very much worth examining at this point, as providing good background for chapters 3 and 4, is *Feit v. Leasco* 332 F. Supp. 544 (E.D.N.Y. 1971), which brings in interesting considerations of the 'common good'.

Feit was one among many shareholders of Reliance Insurance Company ('Reliance') who was persuaded to accept a tender offer of shares of Leasco in a successful takeover. Leasco wished to gain control over Reliance because through research it had discovered that Reliance possessed over $100MM of 'surplus surplus', that is to say, of capital over and above what might reasonably be thought to be needed to cover even an extraordinary rise in insurance claims. This 'surplus surplus' was the reason for the takeover. It was apparently known to a few analysts but not known by Reliance shareholders. Leasco failed to disclose its existence, or its plans for use of the surplus after the takeover. Its management was found guilty of violating the Securities Acts for concealing or omitting material facts and ordered to pay recovery money damages.

The case raised issues of disclosure and materiality, because it was alleged that Leasco had not disclosed material facts. The case is relevant for accounting ethics as helping to define the role of auditing and accounting in financial markets. Accountants are the ordinary agents and certifiers of the disclosures of publicly traded companies.

The court proposed a general conception of the marketplace as a manner of association in which 'insiders' and 'outsiders' buy and sell on a level playing field: "The prospective purchaser of a new issue of securities is entitled to know what the deal is all about. Given an honest and open statement, adequately warning of the possibilities of error and miscalculation and not designed for puffing, the outsider and the insider are placed on more equal grounds for arms length dealing. Such equalization of bargaining power through sharing of knowledge in the securities market is a basic national policy underlying the federal securities laws."

The primary purpose of those laws is "to place potential securities purchasers on a parity with their vendors to the extent practicable". This claim then serves as the basis of the court's rejection of the defendants' claim that the disclosure of the surplus surplus was not material, on the grounds that Leasco's offer to exchange was so attractive, that it would have been accepted by Reliance shareholders even if they knew about that surplus surplus. What is important for materiality, the court maintains, is not that a reasonable investor would have decided otherwise, had he known of the fact, but rather that the fact is the sort of thing that a reasonable investor would have wanted to know about and to be able to take into account, in making his decision— even if he would have decided in the same way. Materiality thus needs to be determined relative to this ideal of a market as displaying 'parity'. In no way can the investor be *manipulated* or *forced* to act; and the investor can be manipulated even if he ends up carrying out the very same purchase or sale that he would have carried out if he had decided fully on his own:

> The solicited Reliance shareholders who received the prospectus in question "ought reasonably to [have been] informed" of an estimate of surplus surplus "before purchasing" the Leasco package. 17 C.F.R. § 230.405(l). It was a fact which these investors needed to "make an intelligent, informed decision whether or not to buy the security." *Escott v. BarChris Construction Corp.*, 283 F. Supp. 643, 681 (S.D.N.Y. 1968). It was a matter which had "an important bearing upon the nature or condition * * * or * * * business" of Reliance tending to deter

acceptance of the exchange offer (id.) and "which in reasonable and objective contemplation might [have affected] the value of [Reliance's] stock." *Kohler v. Kohler*, 319 F.2d 634, 642 (7th Cir. 1963). See *Chasins v. Smith, Barney & Co.*, 438 F.2d 1167, 1171 (2d Cir. 1971); *SEC v. Texas Gulf Sulphur*, 401 F.2d 833, 849 (2d Cir. 1968), cert. denied sub nom. *Coates v. SEC* and *Kline v. SEC*, 394 U.S. 976, 89 S. Ct. 1454, 22 L. Ed. 2d 756 (1969); *List v. Fashion Park*, 340 F.2d 457, 462 (2d Cir.), cert. denied sub nom. *List v. Lerner*, 382 U.S. 811, 86 S. Ct. 23, 15 L. Ed. 2d 60, rehearing denied, 382 U.S. 933, 86 S. Ct. 305, 15 L. Ed. 2d 344 (1965). It was a fact to which "a reasonable man would attach importance in determining" whether to accept the Leasco exchange offer. *List v. Fashion Park*, supra at 462.

Given this general conception of the market place as involving parity and fairness, then disclosure becomes important for two reasons. First, it protects the investor, a major aim of the Securities Acts of 1933 and 1934:

The ultimate goal of the Securities Act is, of course, investor protection. Effective disclosure is merely a means. The entire legislative scheme can be frustrated by technical compliance with the requirements of the Securities and Exchange Commission's Form S-1 for preparation of registration statements in the absence of any real intent to communicate. It is for this reason that the SEC, through its rule making power, has consistently required "clearly understandable" prospectuses.

Much less important for the court is the effect that a requirement to disclose has upon business practices (which, observe, is essentially a consequentialist consideration):

The second — and for our purposes less important — goal of the full disclosure policy is deterrence. This consideration arose from excesses of the 1920's and the havoc subsequently wreaked on investors. The drafters accepted as an article of faith and common sense that if management must bare all on pain of civil and criminal liability its dirty intra-corporate linen will be cleaned before the registration statement is filed.

Concomitantly, such disclosure has the prophylactic effect of promoting general business integrity.

In conclusion, *Feit v. Leasco* offers a striking explication of the sort of good judgment that would be required in an accountant, to have a good sense of the requirements of disclosure and materiality.   A prospectus discloses properly, only if it promotes the aims of the securities laws, and something it includes or omits can be judged to be material, only in relation to an abstract ideal of the fair positioning and equitability of the investor, vis-à-vis the management of a company and other 'insiders'. This is an excellent example of how the 'association' which is the marketplace is governed by relevant laws aiming to preserve its fairness, and an accountant can exercise good judgment in this domain, only through attention to the purpose of that association and its common good, as safeguarded by law.

Chapter 3 Review
Learning Objectives and Review Questions

Learning Objectives

After reading this chapter you should be able to:
• Distinguish the principal types of ethical theory.
• Explain the classical understanding of goodness and virtue.
• Distinguish intellectual virtue from virtue of character.
• Identify the cardinal virtues.
• Explain what a 'common good' is.
• Explain the basic purpose of law in any association.

Questions for Review

1. Which of the following activities is not ethically neutral?
   a. Paying one's monthly bills
   b. Driving to work
   c. Talking with friends
   d. All of the above
2. Which of the following is not a major theory of ethics?
   a. Consequentialism
   b. Kantianism
   c. Virtue ethics
   d. Modern ethics
3. Which of the following is not a reason why consequentialism is unsatisfactory?
   a. Consequentialism regards all moral reasoning as instrumental, means-end reasoning.
   b. Consequentialism holds that slavery might in some circumstances be right.
   c. Whether we do well or not in how we think is typically not a matter of its consequences.
   d. Consequentialism is too abstract to apply without relying upon other substantive moral principles.

4. Which of the following sorts of actions would be especially difficult to evaluate using the Categorical Imperative?

    a. Whether to cheat on one's taxes.

    b. How to resolve an argument with one's spouse.

    c. Whether to ignore a red light when driving.

    d. Whether killing animals is wrong.

    e. Both a. and b.

    f. Both b. and d.

5. Complete the sentence: Something is good if _____.

    a. Someone likes or desires it.

    b. People think that it is good.

    c. It has traits those that enable it to carry out its task well.

    d. It brings happiness to people.

6. The characteristic work of a thing should be understood as:

    a. What people use it for.

    b. What it alone can do.

    c. What it can do better than other things.

    d. What it does constantly and without ceasing.

    e. Both a. and b.

    f. Both a. and c.

    g. Both b. and c.

7. True of false: It is possible to acquire the virtues simply by taking a course in ethics.

8. Which of the following would be the typical way of acquiring integrity?

    a. Taking a course on integrity.

    b. Acting with integrity in small matters.

    c. Learning a definition of integrity.

    d. Seeing good examples of integrity.

9. When (as in the example in the text) a farmer joins a militia dedicated to the common defense, his membership in the association involves reciprocity, because in exchange for the protection that the militia provides, which is what he receives, he gives up:

    a. His right to defend his homestead for himself.

    b. His life.

    c. His natural authority over himself.

    d. His money.

10. Our term 'ethics' is derived from the Greek word for:
    a. habit
    b. morality
    c. divine worship
    d. law

11. True or false: According to the court in *Feit v. Leasco*, an omission is material only if, had the information been included, a substantial number of investors who relied on that information would have acted differently.

Suggested Answers

1. d. Although some kinds of actions are ethically neutral, in the sense that they are neither right nor wrong intrinsically, every particular action that we do is either done correctly and appropriately or not, and thus it is good or bad and not 'ethically neutral'. Note that for an action to be done correctly it need not be done deliberately. In fact, some actions are correct only if not (in any ordinary sense) deliberate, e.g. good conversation when watching a football game on television with friends. Human actions are typically good.

2. d. Modern theories of ethics include Consequentialism and Kantianism.

3. d. This is an objection that holds, rather, of Kantianism. Consequentialism is attractive and finds adherents precisely because it is not abstract but rather promises to make moral deliberation a precise matter of calculation.

4. f. How to resolve an argument with one's spouse frequently involves matters that have to do with one's particular relationship with one's spouse. But judgments about these matters are typically not universalizable. Whether killing animals is wrong requires a judgment as to whether animals are equal moral subjects with human beings. But a substantive judgment of that sort is presupposed by Kantianism and not therefore decidable by its 'formalism'.

5. c. This is an application of the principle that goodness, virtue, and distinctive work are interdefined.

6. g.   Classically, and going back to Plato, it was held that the characteristic work of a thing can be identified by looking to what that sort of thing alone can do, or what that sort does better than any other kind of thing.

7. False.   A virtue involving character needs to be acquired by doing actions that are typical of that virtue.   It is acquired by appropriate action, not by mere thinking.

8. b.   Since integrity involves motivation and therefore character, it needs to be acquired by appropriate action and not by mere thinking. But the best way to grow in a trait we do not already have is to do actions regarding matters that are analogous, and typically little things or first things are the best analogues.

9. a.   In any association the members must forsake their right to pursue the relevant good privately.   (Of course, the respects or extent in which they must do this are implied by the nature and law of the association.)

10. a.   The term 'ethics' applied originally to human character (which, it was thought, was constituted by various habits), and from there it has been expanded to apply to matters of right and wrong generally.

11. False.   It's not necessary that they would (in fact, predictably) have acted differently; it's enough if they might reasonably have wanted to take that information into account before deciding.

4

Basics of Accounting Ethics

IN THIS CHAPTER we examine the ethical reasons for the key ethical
ideals of the profession of accounting. After considering why accounting
is a profession at all, we discuss what constitutes a practitioner's
integrity; what it means to act with due regard for the public interest;
and what independence and objectivity amount to, and how they are
related. We emphasize that none of these ideals can flourish outside of
an appropriate culture. We conclude by looking at the ideal for an
accountant that was proposed in *U.S. v. Arthur Young.*

Professionalism

"Obviously no one can claim to be a member of a profession, or
expect to succeed in one, unless he is prepared, when necessary,
to subordinate his own interest to that of his client."—George
Oliver May (in "The Accountant and the Investor", 1932)

"The high-minded accountant who undertakes to practice in
this field assumes high ethical obligations, and it is the
assumption of such obligations that makes what might otherwise
be a business, a profession. Of all the group of professions which
are closely allied with business, there is none in which the
practitioner is under a greater ethical obligation to persons who

are not his immediate clients; and it is for this reason I believe accounting ought, and can be made, to take an outstanding position in this group."—Ibid.

The first article of the AICPA Principles of Professional Conduct draws attention to the fact that accounting is a profession:

52.01 As professionals, certified public accountants perform an essential role in society. Consistent with that role, members of the American Institute of Certified Public Accountants have responsibilities to all those who use their professional services. Members also have a continuing responsibility to cooperate with each other to improve the art of accounting, maintain the public's confidence, and carry out the profession's special responsibilities for self-governance. The collective efforts of all members are required to maintain and enhance the traditions of the profession.

It is therefore worth reflecting on what a profession is, how a profession is set apart from an ordinary business, and why ethical standards are essential to professionalism.

A profession is distinct from a business because it aims at a good that is incommensurably higher than the goods and services of the marketplace. Each business is an association (see previous chapter), which has as its goal the common production or achievement of some good, to be sold for profit. Any good to which a price is attached is *ipso facto* made commensurate with any other such good. Two goods are commensurable if it is meaningful to say that the one good has a value that is some multiple of the other good. For instance, a sneaker manufacturer sells running shoes for $80; a stocking company sells quality nylon stockings for $20: therefore it is meaningful to say that each pair of sneakers is worth four nylon stockings. The goods are in this way commensurable.

> Commensurability: Two goods are commensurable, if it is meaningful to say that the one good has a value that is some multiple of the other good.

But not all goods are commensurable. Roughly, any good which is an instrument or provides for some comfort or assistance to the body, its appearance or needs, is commensurable with any other good of that class: food; clothing; shelter; transportation; cosmetics; etc. Call these 'instrumental' goods'.

> Instrumental good: Any good which serves as an instrument or provides some comfort or assistance to the body, its appearance or needs.

But there are some goods that have a value that cannot be measured in terms of instrumental goods. Health is obviously of that sort: good health is not on the same level as instrumental goods, because good health is a precondition for enjoying any instrumental good at all. Other goods that are incommensurable with instrumental goods are such things as knowledge; human rights; freedom; justice; religious worship. Call these 'honorable' goods (from the Latin, *bonum honestum*). It is a mark of a profession that it aims at a good of that sort, which is incommensurably higher than instrumental goods. A business aims at instrumental goods; a profession aims at goods that instrumental goods are for, or which are a precondition of instrumental goods being goods at all. Thus, teaching; medicine; public service; and law are professions.

> Honorable good (*bonum honestum*): Any good which is what instrumental goods are for, or which is a precondition of an instrumental good being good at all.

Accounting is a profession because it aims at *knowledge*, insofar as it verifies that some presentation of the position of a company is accurate and representative; and because the *trust* which accounting makes possible is a precondition of the good operation of the marketplace (call this the 'public trust'). Knowledge and trust are not instrumental goods; therefore, accounting is a profession.

We can formulate a list of professions corresponding to identifiable honorable goods:

'Honorable good'	*Corresponding Profession*
Knowledge	Teacher/Professor/Researcher
Justice	Law
Health	Medicine
Freedom, Rights	Public Service
Public Trust	Accounting

Integrity

"It is painful to have to disagree with those by whom one has been retained, and the person in whose interest one does so is unlikely ever to know what has been done or to appreciate the stand that has been taken on his behalf. But in the long run, the willingness of an accountant to do what he conceives to be his duty to the unknown investor, even if by so doing he alienates a client and suffers a present loss of business, brings a rich reward both in self-respect and in a professional reputation which, in turn, brings a pecuniary benefit."—George Oliver May (in "The Accountant and the Investor", 1932)

There are various characteristics of a profession that follow from the fact that professions aim at goods incommensurably higher than instrumental goods. These three characteristics capture what is called the 'integrity' which an accountant is expected to show. Integrity is a mark of any professional, but, as the quotation from May above indicates, in some special ways it applies to the profession of accounting.

1) *A professional supplies disinterested service.* The payment that a professional receives for services has more of the character of an honorarium or stipend than a strict equivalent. Strictly, the work of a professional cannot be compensated for by money, because money is only an instrumental good, but a professional provides an incommensurably higher good. It is because a professional's services have this character that self-interest, in the form of economic advancement, should be an incidental aim in the work of a professional, and a professional should always be prepared, as maintained in the quotation above, to sacrifice self-interest to attain the good that he or

she aims to provide. Those who are principally served by a professional sometimes are unable to repay at all, and in some cases do not even know that they have received a service. A professional is in this sense essentially altruistic. (See May's comment above that an accountant, in serving investors, is "under a greater ethical obligation to persons who are not his immediate clients.")

2) *A professional is self-regulating.* A professional is essentially self-regulating.[20] Contrast this with someone who provides an instrumental good. Such a person is strictly working at the service and on the demand of someone else. If Jones is providing sneakers to Smith in exchange for stockings, then the stockings have to be made to Jones' specification; and Jones is free to do what he wants with them, even destroy them, once he has acquired them. But because the good provided by a professional is incommensurably higher than an instrumental good, then the client has no authority to specify it; rather, it is 'honored' and shown due respect by the professional in how he or she pursues it. (This is what the AICPA Code refers to as "the profession's special responsibilities for self-governance".)

Note that a profession is self-regulating both corporately and individually. It is self-regulating corporately, insofar as a profession is and should be ultimately responsible for setting and enforcing high standards of behavior among its practitioners. It is self-regulating individually, because (as we saw in Chapter 2), a professional must constantly rely on his or her judgment in applying the ethical principles of the professional to daily circumstances. As the AICPA Principles state: "Integrity is measured in terms of what is right and just. In the absence of specific rules, standards, or guidance, or in the face of conflicting opinions, a member should test decisions and deeds by asking: 'Am I doing what a person of integrity would do? Have I retained my integrity?' Integrity requires a member to observe both the form and the spirit of technical and ethical standards; circumvention of those standards constitutes subordination of judgment" 54.03.

---

[20] It is instructive to note that the PCAOB was not established as a government agency, but effectively as an association accountable to the SEC for which membership is voluntary—if one desires to do SEC audit work.

3) *A professional is essentially ethical in his or her work and outlook.* Because a profession aims at a good that is incommensurably higher than an instrumental good, the entire orientation and outlook of a professional should be such that it attests to the priority of that good and of other 'honorable' goods, over instrumental goods. Thus, the entire orientation and outlook of a professional has to be marked by a recognition of the priority, in particular, of ethical considerations over monetary benefit. This is why the AICPA Code, in the Preamble to its statement of Principles, remarks that: "The Principles call for an unswerving commitment to honorable behavior, even at the sacrifice of personal advantage", 51.02). The good that a profession provides is indistinguishable from the ethical commitment of those who provide it.

> The three characteristics of integrity, belonging to any profession are:
> 1. Disinterested service.
> 2. Self-regulation, both corporately and personally.
> 3. Interweaving of ethical commitment and professional service.

These three characteristics apply to accounting to a very high degree:
• Disinterested service—especially because, as we said, those helped by an accountant ('the public') can include persons quite remote from and unknown to the accountant.
• Self-regulation—especially because accounting involves arriving at a reasonable judgment, when taking into account the reasonability of the judgments of a variety of well-informed persons (management; consultants; audit committee; legal counsel).
• Interweaving of ethical commitment and professional service—especially because the good provided through the work of an accountant, trust, is itself ethical in character.

Public Interest

"I would not have you think that because the investor is not his immediate client the accountant owes nothing to the investor except legal duties and ethical obligations. This is not, of course, the fact. It is to the investor that he owes his entire practice in the field of financial auditing, and it is only because the investor exists and attaches weight to an accountant's report that the banker employs the accountant's services in this field. And the continued success of the accountant is dependent on his retaining the confidence of the investing public. An enlightened self-interest, therefore, as well as self-respect, calls for the maintenance of a proper ethical standard by the practitioner."—George Oliver May (in "The Accountant and the Investor", 1932)

In Chapter 3 we introduced the notion of a 'characteristic activity' or 'distinctive work' of a thing, and we said that something is good, if it has those traits that enable it to carry out its distinctive work well. The traits that enable a thing to carry out its distinctive work are its 'virtues'.

In the same way, the 'virtues' of an accountant can be understood in relation to the distinctive work of an accountant. The 'virtues' of an accountant are important, because they constitute a goal and standard of action: they set down what one looks for in an accountant, and what constitutes a 'high standard' of behavior for an accountant.

An accountant's 'distinctive work' is of course varied. For instance, what a practitioner aims to accomplish in a compilation is different from a review, which in turn is different from an audit. Consider the following standard definitions of these tasks:

Compilation: the use of accounting expertise (as opposed to auditing expertise) in order to collect, classify, and summarize financial information.

Review: the use of auditing expertise in a limited manner (that is, involving procedures which do not provide all of the evidence that would be required in an audit) to reach the judgment that nothing has been found which would indicate that the financial statements of a firm are not prepared, in all material respects, in accordance with some accepted financial reporting framework.

Audit: the use of audit expertise to assert whether the financial statements of a firm are prepared, in all

material respects, in accordance with some accepted
financial reporting framework, so as to present fairly, in
all material respects, the position of that firm.

But although these tasks are different, they have something in common.
Generally, the task of an accountant is to provide credibility and
assurance—in the case of a compilation, 'internal' assurance to the firm,
as regards its own information; in the more important case of a review or
audit, assurance (of varying degrees) to a third party, typically a creditor
or investor. Thus, an accountant allows one party to rely upon the
reports of another party. An accountant provides the conditions for
trust, and trust is essential for the fair and free operation of the market.
This is the 'distinctive work' or contribution of an accountant.

> The distinctive work or contribution of an accountant is
> securing the conditions of trust.

This distinctive work is what is meant by the phrase 'public interest'.
Thus the AICPA Code includes the following:

A distinguishing mark of a profession is acceptance of its
responsibility to the public. The accounting profession's public
consists of clients, credit grantors, governments, employers,
investors, the business and financial community, and others who
rely on the objectivity and integrity of certified public
accountants to maintain the orderly functioning of commerce.
This reliance imposes a public interest responsibility on
certified public accountants (53.01).

It then becomes clear what the 'virtues' of an accountant are. These are
the traits that enable an accountant to inspire trust. In order to inspire
trust, it is clear that an accountant must:

1. Maintain himself or herself in circumstances in which there
are not any inducements or incentives to misrepresent the
financial position of a firm.

2. Have sufficient skill to be able to assess and make a judgment
about the represented financial position of a firm.

3. Seek information and carry out the investigation to the extent
that is necessary, in view of his

4. Having a concern with what a creditor or investor would find relevant; and then

5. Actually arriving at a fair and a reasonable judgment as regards the represented financial position of a firm; and,

6. Expressing this judgment in language which allows a third party naturally to form the same judgment.

And from these we arrive at the accepted ideals of accounting:

1. is a Concern for Maintaining Independence.

2. is Competence.

3. is Due Care.

4. is a Sense of the Public Interest.

5. and 6. are Objectivity.

Concern for Independence and Competence are virtues that make it possible to carry out a good review or audit at all. Independence is technically a condition rather than a virtue: it is the condition of not having inducements or incentives that would deflect one's judgment. But there is a virtue which consists of the settled intention of maintaining independence, and of valuing independence, even when doing so involves a sacrifice or is detrimental to self-interest, which may be called a 'Concern for Maintaining Independence'. Competence is of course professional expertise. It has a sister-virtue, which might be called, 'Respect for One's Own Limits', a form of humility, because a good practitioner not only has the competence to carry out those engagements he or she undertakes, but also has the self-knowledge to see when an engagement should not be undertaken, because of a lack of sufficient expertise.

Due Care is a virtue that shows itself in the course of a review or audit. This is the virtue that enables a practitioner to seek (as we saw in Chapter 2) what information is reasonably required for arriving at a sound judgment.

A Sense of the Public Interest involves being able to regard the review or audit from the point of view of a concerned third-party, with respect to whom a representation in a financial report would be material or not. A Sense of the Public Interest helps a practitioner judge what precautions are required by Due Care.

Objectivity is a soundness in judgment that can be exercised only after the other conditions are in place. It implies transparency in disclosure, that is, a truthfulness of expression, which consists in an effective concern to cause or lead another interested party to form a truthful judgment about the financial condition of a company.

Furthermore, as we saw, Integrity is also a virtue, or rather the foundation of all of the virtues of an accountant, as being the basic attitude of service of a professional.

> The six distinctive virtues of an accountant:
> Concern for Maintaining Independence
> Competence and Sense of Limits
> Due Diligence (Due Care)
> Sense of the Public Interest
> Objectivity (Sound Judgment)
> Integrity (Professionalism)

Independence

"To be willing to exercise his judgment objectively and dispassionately, the accountant must be a man of high character, prepared to recognize and observe high ethical obligations even to his own immediate disadvantage. To be able to do so he must be free from any relation to the subject matter or to the parties in interest which might cloud his judgment or impair his loyalty to the investors to whom his paramount duty is owed."— George Oliver May (in "The Accountant and the Investor", 1932)

"As a practical rule, an accountant should run no risk of putting himself in a position where his interest might with any reason be thought to be large enough to affect his judgment, and it is the part of wisdom to resolve all doubts on such a question conservatively by declining the doubtful appointment". —*Ibid*.

As mentioned, strictly speaking, 'independence' is a condition in which an accountant finds himself. It is the condition of not having or experiencing inducements or incentives ('temptations') to render an incorrect judgment (that is, a judgment lacking in objectivity). The disposition or frame of mind by which an accountant actively seeks to preserve the condition of independence might best be called a 'Concern for Maintaining Independence'. See AICPA Code 55.03: "...the maintenance of objectivity and independence requires a continuing assessment of client relationships and public responsibility.'

> Independence (the condition): The condition of being free of incentives or inducements that would work to deflect judgment.
>
> Independence (the virtue): Valuing independence (the condition) above one's own interests and habitually taking care to achieve independence.

There are both external and internal factors that can destroy independence. The external factors are those that are more commonly studied and are more familiar. These are so-called 'conflicts of interest'. A clear and egregious example would be: a practitioner has a material (for him) investment in a company that he is auditing and therefore would benefit if the company's financial condition were represented well.

An internal factor would be some extreme or exaggerated desire, of the sort that would make someone prone to alter his or her judgment, in circumstances which would not ordinarily constitute a 'conflict of interest'. For instance, suppose it is granted that, when a firm that is engaged to audit a company also receives large consulting fees from that company, this does not *ipso facto* imply a conflict of interest—nonetheless, if the auditors have an extreme or exaggerated desire for money (that is, 'greed'), then their independence would likely be compromised by such an arrangement. That is, internal factors can compromise independence even if, in some sense, it 'shouldn't' be the case that external factors do.

Because there are internal as well as external factors that can compromise independence, it is necessary that an auditor not only keep himself or herself free from conflicts of interest, but also acquire and maintain the sort of character that cannot be deflected from duty because of monetary interests. Good character is therefore a prerequisite of independence.

> External attacks on (the condition of) independence: conflicts of interest.
> Internal attacks on (the condition of) independence: greed; bad character.

It often happens that a practitioner's independence is undermined, and his or her objectivity is affected, without the practitioner consciously being aware of any partiality or incorrectness of judgment. That is to say, as a result of a lack of independence, perhaps unnoticed, the practitioner shows systematic 'bias'. Because it is possible, and indeed easy, to lose independence, without becoming aware that one has lost independence, it follows that, when there are doubtful cases, it is correct to err well on the side of independence. As George Oliver May puts the point so eloquently: "... it is the part of wisdom to resolve all doubts on such a question conservatively".

This is one reason why the traditional and correct standard for a practitioner is to avoid any situation which carries with it even the appearance of a lack of independence. See AICPA Code 55.01: "Independence precludes relationships that *may appear to impair* a member's objectivity in rendering attestation services." See also 55.03: "Such a member who provides auditing and other attestation services should be independent in fact *and appearance*." (Emphases added.)

That this strict standard is required is evident also from a consideration of the distinctive work of an accountant. The accountant distinctively provides trust, and therefore also the conditions of trust. But trust implies trustworthiness, and that someone is trustworthy is a matter of perception. For there to be trust, then, it is not enough that someone simply be trustworthy—he or she must also appear trustworthy. The trustworthiness of an accountant therefore requires the avoidance even of anything that would make accountants seem not to be trustworthy.

> Given that the distinctive work of the accountant involves trust, even the appearance of a lack of independence must be avoided.

That accounting is a profession, corporately so, implies the same result. Each practitioner has a responsibility to maintain the trustworthiness of the profession as a whole. An apparent lack of independence in a particular case, if it concerned that practitioner alone, might perhaps be dismissed as of no consequence, or as the sort of thing that will likely be correctly understood by those who are involved. But since each professional's work affects the public perception of everyone else in that profession, even a putatively isolated or atypical appearance of non-independence becomes important. See AICPA Code 52.01: "Members also have a continuing responsibility *to cooperate with each other* to improve the art of accounting, maintain the public's confidence, and carry out the profession's special responsibilities for self-governance. The *collective efforts* of all members are required to maintain and enhance the traditions of the profession." (Emphases added.)

Objectivity

"I believe that every high-minded accountant has accepted the principle that, once his conclusions are reached, the report or certificate which he issues, and which is designed to influence action, must be so worded that not only will every statement made therein be literally true, but every inference which could legitimately be drawn from the language will be warranted by the facts. There is no place in accountants' certificates for what President Roosevelt once called 'weasel words'." —George Oliver May (in "The Accountant and the Investor", 1932)

One should distinguish objectivity in thought from objectivity of expression. Objectivity in thought is a condition of sound judgment. It is akin to the impartiality, cool-headedness, and fairness that one looks for in an umpire or judge. It is a way of looking at and evaluating evidence, so that all information and every indication is, in one's own mind and deliberations, given the correct weight. The AICPA Code speaks of objectivity in thought as an 'impartial' frame of mind which involves a kind of 'honesty' (see 55.01).

Objectivity of expression is when what one says or writes is naturally and reasonably understood in such a way as that it conveys an accurate representation. Objectivity of expression is what is typically referred to as 'transparency'. A representation of the financial condition of a company is transparent when it naturally suggests what is correct to think about that company's financial position. A transparent communication suggests no more than it is correct to think; and everything that is correct to think it suggests.

> Transparency: a trait of a communication, where what that communication is naturally understood as saying is a fair representation of what one is making a judgment about.

Objectivity implies transparency because the objectivity of an accountant is not some private thought or idea which the practitioner keeps to himself or herself. The very point of an accountant is to provide a report to someone else. Therefore, necessarily, objectivity takes the form of providing a report. But if the report is to someone, then how another person is likely to understand the report becomes decisively important. Objectivity, then, involves not simply making sure that one's own judgment lines up correctly with what one is making a judgment about; it also involves making sure that the judgment that someone else will likely make, based on what one says, will line up correctly with what one is making a judgment about.

> Objectivity in thought: an impartial, honest, and fair state of mind.
> Objectivity of expression: transparency.

The importance of culture for virtue

"The young accountant may find it hard to take the first stand for the principles that have been suggested for his observance, but he will find that this is essentially a case in which 'it is the first step that costs.'" —George Oliver May (in "The Accountant and the Investor", 1932)

Someone who seriously wishes to attain a particular result, has to work back in thought and provide all of the conditions that are required, in order to insure that result. For instance, if someone wants to grow a cornfield, he has to plant corn kernels; but a condition of those kernels' growing is that the field remain free from pests and weeds; and also that the plants be furnished with adequate water.

Similarly, we have seen that, for an accountant to carry out well his or her distinctive work, it is necessary that he or she have the virtues that an accountant should have. But to *have* the virtues one must first *acquire* them; and to acquire them it is necessary that the conditions obtain in which they can be acquired.

The term 'culture' refers to the broad set of conditions that make it easy to acquire certain habits of action and to live in a certain way. Clearly, the establishment of a 'culture' in an accounting firm is not something that can be done by a single practitioner; moreover, this is primarily the responsibility of senior partners—the so-called 'tone at the top'. The historic culture of Arthur Andersen, for instance, which was famous for being scrupulously ethical, and which played a large role in the early success of the firm, was largely the expression of the character of the firm's founder ("...stern, erect, somewhat ascetic, exceedingly proper", according to the *History of Accounting: An International Encyclopedia*, Garland, 1996. It was Andersen's culture of propriety that, arguably, made the firm's commitment to innovation something that was both responsible and sustainable over the long term.)

The correct culture in a firm is a precondition of an accountant's acquiring and persevering in the various virtues described above. An implemented code of ethics is a useful instrument in fostering the correct culture. A code is implemented if: (i) there is some procedure in place which guarantees that practitioners study and understand it; (ii) there are incentives for the good observance of the code; and (iii) the code is 'enforced', that is, practitioners are in the habit of encouraging one another to observe it; they expect others to follow it; and egregious violations are reported and dealt with appropriately. Naturally, there is a chicken-and-egg problem involving any code—those who most need it will be least inclined to implement it. Once again, strong personal character, especially among more senior partners, is irreplaceable.

As we saw in Chapter 3, virtues of character are acquired by doing actions characteristic of those virtues. In practice, that means acting in the right way especially: (i) in small matters; and (ii) in new situations. Acting correctly in small matters establishes patterns of action that carry over into large matters: if someone has not managed to be ethical and principled when the stakes are small, he certainly will not succeed in doing so when the incentives against it are great. Acting correctly in new situations, right from the start, establishes a 'precedent', which subsequent actions are likely to follow. Thus, for instance, how an auditor reacts the very first time she encounters signs of even minor fraud on the part of the management of an audited company will largely settle how the audit will play out subsequently. It is sometimes said that 'second thoughts are best', but in matters of ethics it often happens that conscience speaks clearly and best on the first occasion but later gets dampened.

Illustrative legal case

United States v. Arthur Young, 465 U.S. 805 (1984) concerns whether the auditing firm Arthur Young was required to hand over to the IRS the tax accrual working papers that it had used in estimating contingent tax liability for Amerada Hess Corporation ('Amerada'). In conducting a routine audit of Amerada, the IRS discovered what it regarded as a questionable payment from a 'special disbursement account', after which it began a criminal investigation against Amerada. The IRS issued a summons to Young, to turn over the working papers, and Amerada instructed Young not to do so. A district court ruled the papers 'relevant' to the IRS investigation, pursuant to the relevant law empowering such investigations, and therefore it required Young to surrender the papers. An appeals court agreed with the finding of relevance, but found that the working papers fell under an initial, so-called 'worker product immunity', protecting the working papers and other instruments of an accountant's professional work. This immunity was postulated by the court on analogy with a similar immunity for attorneys recognized by *Hickman v. Taylor*, 329 U.S. 495 (1947). The appeals court determined that the IRS, although it had shown relevance, had not shown sufficient cause to overcome this immunity. The Supreme Court agreed with the lower courts as regards relevance but denied that the working papers of accountants were protected by any 'worker product' immunity.

In denying this sort of immunity, the Supreme Court had to determine, negatively, that the accountant-client relationship was not analogous to the attorney-client relationship, and, positively, that the accountant plays a role that would make that sort of immunity inappropriate. Thus the case is of great importance as setting down in law a characterization of what we have called the 'function' of an accountant. The crucial passage from *Hickman* is the following:

> Historically, a lawyer is an officer of the court and is bound to work for the advancement of justice while faithfully protecting the rightful interests of his clients. In performing his various duties, however, it is essential that a lawyer work with a certain degree of privacy, free from unnecessary intrusion by opposing parties and their counsel. Proper preparation of a client's case demands that he assemble information, sift what he considers to be the relevant from the irrelevant facts, prepare his legal theories and plan his strategy without undue and needless interference. That is the historical and the necessary way in which lawyers act within the framework of our system of jurisprudence to promote justice and to protect their clients' interests

Note that *Hickman* fashions the immunity on the presumption that a lawyer is acting in a certain confidence "protecting the rightful interests of his clients" and in order "to protect [the] client's interests". That is, that an attorney essentially has a fiduciary relationship to the client.

This is the very point that the Supreme Court denies as regards accountants:

> The *Hickman* work-product doctrine was founded upon the private attorney's role as the client's confidential adviser and advocate, a loyal representative whose duty it is to present the

client's case in the most favorable possible light. An independent certified public accountant performs a different role. By certifying the public reports that collectively depict a corporation's financial status, the independent auditor assumes a public responsibility transcending any employment relationship with the client. The independent public accountant performing this special function owes ultimate allegiance to the corporation's creditors and stockholders, as well as to the investing public. This "public watchdog" function demands that the accountant maintain total independence from the client at all times and requires complete fidelity to the public trust. To insulate from disclosure a certified public accountant's interpretations of the client's financial statements would be to ignore the significance of the accountant's role as a disinterested analyst charged with public obligations.

We cannot accept the view that the integrity of the securities markets will suffer absent some protection for accountants' tax accrual work-papers. The Court of Appeals apparently feared that, were the IRS to have access to tax accrual work-papers, a corporation might be tempted to withhold from its auditor certain information relevant and material to a proper evaluation of its financial statements. But the independent certified public accountant cannot be content with the corporation's representations that its tax accrual reserves are adequate; the auditor is ethically and professionally obligated to ascertain for himself as far as possible whether the corporation's contingent tax liabilities have been accurately stated. If the auditor were convinced that the scope of the examination had been limited by management's reluctance to disclose matters relating to the tax accrual reserves, the auditor would be unable to issue an unqualified opinion as to the accuracy of the corporation's financial statements. Instead, the auditor would be required to issue a qualified opinion, an adverse opinion, or a disclaimer of opinion, thereby notifying the investing public of possible potential problems inherent in the corporation's financial reports. Responsible corporate management would not risk a qualified evaluation of a corporate taxpayer's financial posture to afford cover for questionable positions reflected in a prior tax return. Thus, the independent auditor's obligation to serve the public interest assures that the integrity of the securities markets will be preserved, without the need for a work-product immunity for accountants' tax accrual work-papers.

Note that, as in *Feit v. Leasco*, the court first gives an argument based on the nature of accounting, and then argues from the consequences of the doctrine. The court's phrase, "a public responsibility transcending any employment relationship with the client", refers to what we have identified as the attitude of professionalism for accountants. The claim that "The independent public accountant performing this special function owes ultimate allegiance to the corporation's creditors and stockholders, as well as to the investing public" corresponds exactly to what we have identified as Concern for the Public Interest. What the court refers to as the "'public watchdog' function" is exactly what we have referred to as the function of an accountant as providing the indispensable conditions of trust for the sound operation of the marketplace. This 'function' or 'distinctive activity', as we saw, is the basis from which one can deduce the distinctive virtues of an accountant. Note finally that the court's determination that the denial of any 'worker product immunity' for an accountant's working paper would best contribute to full disclosure by companies is based on the presumption that accountants adhere to their 'ethical and professional' obligation "to ascertain for [themselves] as far as possible whether the corporation's contingent tax liabilities have been accurately stated".

Chapter 4 Review
Learning Objectives and Review Questions

Learning Objectives:

After reading this chapter you should be able to:
• Explain the incommensurability of goods.
• Explain what a profession is, and why accounting is a profession.
• Identify the principal virtues of an accountant and relate these to the Code of Professional Conduct.
• Explain the ideals of Integrity, Independence, and Objectivity in relation to the distinctive work of an accountant.
• Distinguish the intellectual virtues from the virtues of character needed in an accountant.
• Characterize the distinctive work of an accountant as described by the United States Supreme Court.

Questions for Review

1. Complete the following quotation: "The high-minded accountant who undertakes to practice in this field assumes high ethical obligations, and it is the assumption of such obligations that makes what might otherwise be a business, _____ ".
    a. An enjoyable vocation.
    b. A high calling.
    c. A profession.
    d. A highly profitable business.
2. Which of the following implies that a good is instrumental?
    a. It has a meaningful price in dollars.
    b. It is worth some multiple of a pair of sneakers.
    c. It is useful for the care of the body.
    d. It can be found in a tool chest.
    e. All of the above.

3. Complete the following quotation: "But in the long run, the willingness of an accountant to do what he conceives to be his duty to _____, even if by so doing he alienates a client and suffers a present loss of business, brings a rich reward both in self-respect and in a professional reputation which, in turn, brings a pecuniary benefit."

    a. his firm

    b. the unknown investor

    c. the issuing house

    d. his country

4. True or false. In reality, an accountant's salary is of the nature of an honorarium.

5. Which of the following is not a component of professional integrity?

    a. Self-regulation

    b. Restrictions on advertising

    c. Disinterested service

    d. Interweaving of ethics and service

6. Complete the following quotation: "It is to _____ that an accountant owes his entire practice in the field of financial auditing."

    a. the SEC

    b. the investor

    c. the shrewd banker

    d. the founders of the big firms

7. The phrase 'public interest' indicates at least the following:

    a. the prime lending rate

    b. the common good

    c. the orderly functioning of commerce

    d. peace and tranquility

8. Independence, the virtue, is to be distinguished from independence, the_____:

    a. condition

    b. result

    c. affirmation

    d. hypothesis

9. Which of the following is not a reason why even the appearance of a lack of independence should be avoided by an accountant?

a. The apparent lack of independence of one practitioner can affect the reputation of all.

b. There is no trust without the appearance of trustworthiness.

c. Someone can lose independence without being aware of it.

d. In accounting as in politics, appearance is reality.

10. The broad set of conditions that make it easy to acquire certain habits of action and to live in a certain way is _____.

a. morality

b. ethics

c. a code of conduct

d. culture

11. True or false. In *U.S. v. Arthur Young*, the Supreme Court held that accountants owe ultimate allegiance to the company which hires them to do an audit.

Suggested answers

1. c. This quotation from George Oliver May succinctly captures what makes a line of work a profession.

2. e. Non-instrumental goods do not have exact (or 'meaningful') dollar equivalents; neither are they exactly commensurable with any instrumental good, such as sneakers; and they broadly pertain to the human mind and 'heart' rather than the body. Of course any instrument in the strict sense, such as a tool found in a tool box, is an instrumental good.

3. b. This quotation from William Oliver May nicely captures the orientation of altruistic service that is inherent in accounting as a profession.

4. True. Because the good that an accountant provides is not an instrumental good, it has no exact monetary equivalent, and his or her compensation is (in reality) more of the nature of an appropriate sign of gratitude and appreciation.

5. b. Restrictions on advertising flow from the fact that an accountant is a professional (and therefore not hawking instrumental goods in the marketplace) but they are not contained in the notion of professional integrity per se.

6. b. Again, another apt quotation from George Oliver May, this time drawing attention to how (as in all sound human relationships) there is really a *reciprocity* between an accountant and the public interest which he or she serves.

7. c. One might think that it also indicates the 'common good', that is, the common good of society in general (of 'political society'), but strictly this is the concern of public servants; an accountant aims to promote and safeguard simply one dimension, albeit an important dimension, of the common good of political society.

8. a. Generally, virtues see to it that good conditions obtain. Independence of competing interests is a good condition for an accountant, because it is necessary if his or her judgment is to be properly objective. But a personal virtue is required, if a person is to act effectively and reliably so as to preserve this good condition in his or her professional work, and this personal virtue is independence, the virtue.

9. d. To hold that 'appearance is reality' is to adopt an attitude incompatible with the objectivity (and therefore regard for truth) which is essential to an accountant's good performance of his or her professional work.

10. d. Culture (and the term is typically used in the sense of 'good culture', although strictly there can be bad forms of culture as well) has aptly been defined as 'society's making it easy to be good'.

11. False. The Supreme Court in *Arthur Young* rather reaffirmed the principle of accounting professional ethics, that an accountant, who serves the public interest, therefore plays the role of a 'public watchdog'.

5

Enron, a Failure of Objectivity and Independence

"EMPLOYEES OF ENRON CORP., its subsidiaries, and its affiliated companies (collectively called the 'Company') are charged with conducting their business affairs in accordance with the highest ethical standards. An employee shall not conduct himself or herself in a manner which directly or indirectly would be detrimental to the best interests of the Company or in a manner which would bring to the employee financial gain separately derived as a direct consequence of his or her employment with the Company. Moral as well as legal obligations will be fulfilled openly, promptly, and in a manner which will reflect pride on the Company's name."—From the *Enron Code of Ethics* (July 2000), in the subsection entitled "Business Ethics".

Background

The Enron story is by now familiar. A company which at the start of 2001 employed 25,000 people and was the 7th largest U.S. company by revenues—voted by readers of *Fortune* magazine as one of the most admired and innovative companies in the country—after a restatement of November 8, 2001, which recognized 1.2 billion dollars of theretofore hidden debt, filed for bankruptcy on December 2, 2001.

Enron's collapse was caused by accounting improprieties. It used Special Purpose Entities ('SPE's, also know as 'Special Purpose

Vehicles') to transfer 'off-balance sheet' about 40 billion dollars of assets; to manipulate earnings; and to hide debt. Because many of these SPEs were not truly independent, either in control or in financing—they were managed, directly or indirectly, by Enron employees, and funded, directly or indirectly, almost solely by Enron stock—they should not, for accounting purposes, have been treated as off-balance sheet, but should have been consolidated.

In its restatement, Enron itself gives a serviceable, if terse, explanation of the irregularity:

> Enron's previously-announced $1.2 billion reduction of shareholders' equity primarily involves the correction of the effect of an accounting error made in the second quarter of 2000 and in the first quarter of 2001. As described in more detail below, four SPEs known as Raptor I-IV (collectively, "Raptor") were created in 2000, permitting Enron to hedge market risk in certain of its investments. (LJM2 invested in these entities, but the related-party nature of the transaction is not relevant to the accounting correction). As part of the capitalization of these entities, Enron issued common stock in exchange for a note receivable. Enron increased notes receivable and shareholders' equity to reflect this transaction. Enron now believes that, under generally accepted accounting principles, the note receivable should have been presented as a reduction to shareholders' equity (similar to a shareholder loan)....
>
> ... In the first quarter of 2001, Enron entered into contracts with Raptor that could have obligated Enron to issue Enron common stock in the future in exchange for notes receivable. Enron accounted for these transactions using the accounting treatment described in the preceding paragraph. This resulted in an additional overstatement of both notes receivable and shareholders' equity by $828 million. As a result of these errors, shareholders' equity and notes receivable were overstated by a total of $1 billion in the unaudited financial statements of Enron at March 31 and June 30, 2001....

The 1.2 billion dollars of additional debt acknowledged in the restatement was not itself crushingly large for Enron—although admittedly Enron's debt-to-capital ratio was close to 50% at the time. The restatement led to Enron's demise because it led to a loss of credibility with Enron's creditors and investors—How much other debt was perhaps hidden by SPEs? What other irregularities were yet to be revealed? How much more of the investing public's confidence in Enron would prove to be unfounded?—Yet this credibility was the very thing sustaining Enron's business.

Although the configuration of the Raptors was extremely complex, the underlying idea was simple—and flawed. Because the Raptors were not truly distinct entities, Enron's transactions with them were sham transactions that the company engaged in with itself. A 'payment' from a Raptor or similar SPE could not possibly count as income; a Raptor or similar SPE could not possibly serve to control risk, lower debt, or hedge losses—any more than an individual can 'pay' himself for services or 'hedge' his own investments. As the Powers report remarked: "The fundamental flaw in these transactions was not that the price was too low [i.e. Enron accepted terms disadvantageous to itself, because one of its own officers was representing the Raptors]. Instead, as a matter of economic substance, it is not clear that anything was really being bought or sold" (Powers report, p. 171).[21] The Raptors and other SPEs had no legitimate business purpose; their sole purpose was to improve the appearance of the health of the company.

Given that these SPE arrangements were viciously circular, and that Enron's dealings with them were sham transactions, how could any intelligent person at Enron have thought they could work? Well, they would have 'worked'—in the sense of hiding Enron's degree of indebtedness, until such time as that presumably improved—if Enron's stock value had continued to increase. If Enron's stock continued to rise, then the SPEs would have remained well 'funded', and presumably the debt that they were designed to hide would have been lowered, over time, by actual payments, or it would have been simply rendered insignificant in relation to Enron's increasing capitalization. But when Enron's stock in fact fell, and dropped below certain limits required for the sham transactions to be viable (about $45/share for the Raptors,

---

[21] The Powers report was a comprehensive investigative report of the Enron collapse, produced for the Enron Board, and published in early 2002.

which was about half of Enron's share price at the beginning of 2001), then the viciously circular character of the SPEs had to be dealt with—and this is what led to Enron's restatement.

There was something of the character of a self-fulfilling prophecy for the SPEs—they would work, just in case they worked. The SPEs hid Enron's debt and allowed the recognition of sham earnings; this in turn made Enron continue to appear to be an attractive company to investors; that it appeared attractive implied a high or increasing share price; that the share price was high or increasing implied that the debt, hidden by the SPEs, could be successfully hidden—which in turn kept Enron appearing attractive. Contrariwise, if the share price of Enron began to fall, then the SPEs would begin to unravel; the debt they hid would be uncovered; this would make Enron appear unattractive, contributing to a greater fall in share price; and so on. Since investors holding shares in Enron would ostensibly be helped by rising share prices, and hurt by falling share prices, it is natural that the 'success' of these SPEs in hiding Enron's debt would seem (misguidedly) a very good thing and even a grave duty to those who devised them.

Enron's use of SPEs is frequently referred to, metaphorically, as a 'shell game'. But this is an inappropriate metaphor. A shell game is a confidence trick, where a ball is quickly moved from shell-to-shell by the con-artist, and then actually removed, by sleight of hand, to be placed deliberately and at will, in some shell not selected by the 'mark'. But the confidence trick to which the Enron SPEs are better likened is a 'Ponzi scheme'. A Ponzi scheme, named after Charles Ponzi, an Italian immigrant to the U.S., is a fraudulent investment operation that involves paying returns to investors out of the money raised from subsequent investors. In 1919-1920, Ponzi claimed to offer returns of up to 400% by taking advantage of an arbitrage that then existed in International Postage Coupons. His business grew from $5,000 in March 1920 to $420,000 in May, to millions in the summer, until eventually it became clear that Ponzi was not buying and selling Postage Coupons at all, but using the surplus of increasing funds invested to pay off past investments (indeed, most of his clients chose to reinvest their profits). Ponzi's 'business' collapsed nearly overnight after a series of critical *Boston Post* stories in the later summer of 1920, which pointed out that there were not even enough postage coupons in existence to justify the amounts that people had invested with him! When Federal agents later raided Ponzi's offices, in fact, they found no postage coupons at all. The profitability of Ponzi's 'business' was based solely on the appearance of its profitability, not on any sound business practice.

And this was largely the situation eighty years later with Enron.

From the investor's point of view

Ponzi was a crude con-artist who, prior to starting his 'business', had worked odd jobs as a waiter and bank clerk and even spent time in prison for forgery and petty crimes. He had no legal advisors; he published no company report or prospectus; his business was never audited. Presumably his business could not have endured a public audit. In contrast, Enron was a public company, and its business was regularly examined and reported upon by Arthur Andersen, historically one of the most prestigious and reliable accounting firms. How could Andersen have signed off on Enron's Ponzi scheme? Well, they not only signed off on it, they helped to design it, and they billed Enron 1.3 million dollars for doing so. To appreciate the wrongness of this, let us approach the matter from the point of view of an investor, the interests of whom, as we have seen, Andersen was charged to serve.

Imagine an investor in middle-America in early March of 2001, burned a bit from the dot.com bust, and wearied by a prolonged bear market, who has cashed out many of his equity positions, but who by that point has regained some of his confidence and is wanting to buy a good growth stock. He picks up the latest issue of *Fortune* magazine and finds there an article by Bethany McLean entitled, "Is Enron Overpriced?". The subheading of the article states, "It's in a bunch of complex businesses. Its financial statements are nearly impenetrable. So why is Enron trading at such a huge multiple?" Our imaginary investor has so far not purchased Enron shares, and Enron stock is expensive, but he wonders whether he isn't 'missing the boat'. Should he now take a position in Enron? Although the stock price, at almost $90, has a p/e ratio of about 55, in late January of 2001 Enron executives met with Wall Street analysts and argued, convincingly to many, that its stock ought really be valued at $126.

In this thought exercise, keep in mind the classic definition of 'materiality'—viz. information about a company is material and should be reported if an investor would reasonably decide to invest or not in that company on the basis of that information.[22]

The article begins by acknowledging Enron's popularity among investors, due largely to Enron's remarkable returns in a relatively dismal investment period. But then McLean raises some concerns. Above all, there is the problem of Enron's debt: in the first 9 months of 2000, Enron's debt increased dramatically by $3.9 billion, making its debt-to-capital ratio now 50%, as opposed to 39% at the end of the previous year. Then there is an apparent problem of cash-flow: during the same period, the company shows nearly a negative cash-flow. But more fundamentally, there is the problem that hardly anyone seems to understand Enron's business: "How exactly does Enron make its money?," McLean wonders, "Details are hard to come by because Enron keeps many of the specifics confidential for what it terms 'competitive reasons.'"

When McLean raises these concerns with Enron executives, they give an apparently plausible explanation:

> But Enron says that extrapolating from its financial statements is misleading. The fact that Enron's cash flow this year was meager, at least when compared with earnings, was partly a result of its wholesale business. Accounting standards mandate that its assets and liabilities from its wholesale business be "marked to market"—valued at their market price at a given moment in time. Changes in the valuation are reported in earnings. But these earnings aren't necessarily cash at the instant they are recorded. [Jeff] Skilling [Enron's CEO] says that Enron can convert these contracts to cash anytime it chooses by "securitizing" them, or selling them off to a financial institution. Enron then receives a "servicing fee," but Skilling says that all the risks (for example, changes in the value of the assets and liabilities) are then transferred to the buyer. That's why, he says, Enron's cash flow will be up dramatically, while debt will be "way

---

[22] Or, more strongly, if the investor would reasonably have wanted to know that information before making up his mind.

down, way down" when the company publishes its full year-end results, which are due out soon.

In retrospect, in this passage it looks as though what Skilling is indirectly referring to is Enron's use of SPEs to 'sell off' risky investments, and he is claiming, in effect, that these structures are capable of resolving any apparent difficulties Enron faces with indebtedness or cash. That is, the SPEs are effectively being relied upon in an argument that investors should purchase Enron stock.

Recall that this is March of 2001. This is Enron's public face. But how did the financial health of the company appear internally? The best evidence we have for this is the famous 'whistle blower' letter of Sherron Watkins, an Enron internal auditor. The letter is sent to the new CEO of Enron, Ken Lay, in August 2001, the day after Skilling's abrupt resignation. "To the layman on the street," Watkins writes, expressing concerns about the true nature of Enron's SPEs, "it will look like we recognized funds flow of $800mm from merchant asset sales in 1999 by selling to a vehicle (Condor) that we capitalized with a promise of Enron stock in later years. Is that really funds flow or is it cash from equity issuance?" As regards Raptor, "It sure looks to the layman on the street that we are hiding losses in a related company and will compensate that company with Enron stock in the future...Raptor looks to be a big bet, if the underlying stocks did well, then no one would be the wiser. If Enron stock did well, the stock issuance to these entities would decline and the transactions would be less noticeable. All has gone against us." She adds, "I am incredibly nervous that we will implode in a wave of accounting scandals....I realize that we have had a lot of smart people looking at this and a lot of accountants including AA & Co. have blessed the accounting treatment. None of that will protect Enron if these transactions are ever disclosed in the bright light of day."

Watkins suggests that her observations were widely appreciated in the company but left largely unstated by those who knew of the SPEs. "I have heard one management level employee from the principle investments group say, 'I know it would be devastating to all of us, but I wish we would get caught. We're such a crooked company.' The principle investments group hedged a large number of their investments with Raptor. These people know and see a lot. Many similar comments are made when you ask about these deals."

Now think again about Skilling's sales-pitch for Enron with McLean of *Fortune* magazine.

Andersen, Independence, and Objectivity

It is natural enough for an executive of a company to promote his company's interests, even if he is aware of grave problems facing the company, and so long as he does not exceed the boundaries of honesty. In a sense, that is his job. But what about that company's auditors, who are in theory independent and have a responsibility to the public interest? Their job is to render an objective report as regards anything within their purview that may be 'material' to an investor's reasonable investment decision. One would expect that, long before the summer of 2001, Andersen auditors would have said to Enron executives, "Look, these SPEs effectively turn Enron into a giant Ponzi scheme. We will not sign off on a financial report which does not consolidate the debt that these SPEs conceal."

In fact, the question of whether to adopt this position seems to have been raised internally by Andersen, in a conference call among 14 of its officers of February 6, 2001, which an internal Andersen memo refers to as an "Enron Retention Meeting". (Keep in mind that the bulk of Andersen documents related to Enron were destroyed in a concerted shredding project of late 2001. What remains is likely to be just a slight indication of the reality.) From the language of the memo, it is clear that the Andersen auditors discussed and shared concerns about the Enron SPEs that were exactly of the character of the (later) Watkins letter:

> A significant discussion was held regarding the related party transactions with LJM [a general name for two Enron SPEs, one of which had ownership in the Raptor SPEs] including the materiality of such amounts to Enron's income statement and the amount retained "off balance sheet".
>
> ...We discussed Enron's reliance on its current credit rating to maintain itself as a high credit rated transaction party.

...We discussed Enron's dependence on transaction execution to meet financial objectives...

...Ultimately the conclusion was reached to retain Enron as a client citing that it appeared that we had the appropriate people and processes in place to serve Enron and manage our engagement risks. We discussed whether there would be a perceived independence issue solely considering our level of fees. We discussed that the concerns should not be on the magnitude of fees but on the nature of fees. We arbitrarily discussed that it would not be unforeseeable that fees could reach a $100 million per year amount considering the multi-disciplinary services being provided. Such amount did not trouble the participants as long as the nature of the services was not an issue.

The decision arrived at by the group was apparently that things should continue as before, since the 'To Do' items at the end of the memo included nothing about challenging the accounting treatment of the SPEs or restating past financials. Rather, action items included such things as making sure the SEC would not have concerns about SPE control (not SPE accounting); placing more responsibility on the Enron Board of Directors; and shifting more responsibility to Enron officers. The items are all procedural. None deal with, or show signs of taking responsibility for, the substantive difficulties evidently raised and discussed in the meeting:

Take away To Do's

Inquire as to whether Andy Fastow [Enron CFO, who effectively controlled the LJM entities] and/or LJM would be viewed as an 'affiliate' from an SEC perspective which would require looking through the transactions and treating them as within the consolidated group.

Suggest that a special committee of the BOD be established to review the fairness of LJM transactions...

Focus on Enron preparing their own documentation and conclusions to issues and transactions.

AA [Arthur Andersen] to focus on timely documentation of final transaction structures to ensure consensus is reached on the final structure.

Note that in the year 2000, Andersen received $25mm in fees for auditing from Enron, and an additional $27mm for consulting services. As mentioned, Andersen helped to structure the Raptor and LJM SPEs, and was paid over $1mm for its work in doing so. Moreover, many internal accountants for Enron were former employees of Andersen. Jeff Skilling in fact was known to have remarked that the best reason for using Andersen as auditors was that they were a good source of talent for recruiting for Enron. (Sherron Watkins was an Andersen accountant, hired by Enron in 1993.)

In light of these facts, it would be reasonable to hold that Andersen was incapable of maintaining the independence that is required of auditors. As we saw, this concern was raised in the Andersen phone conference: "We discussed whether there would be a perceived independence issue solely considering our level of fees." Put aside the consideration that there were issues of independence that arose from other matters besides simply the level of fees. For our purposes, note the fuzziness in even this language. A "perceived independence issue" might mean either:

(a.) The perception, that is, the thought or judgment, that Andersen lacked independence;

(b.) The appearance (to a reasonable observer, aware of the relevant facts) of a lack of independence.

The ambiguity is important, because (a.) is defeasible, but (b.) is not. Someone might judge or think, "Andersen is not independent in its Enron engagement" and be wrong about that. And this is the line of thought taken by the Andersen accountants in the conference call. Recall: "We discussed that the concerns should not be on the magnitude of fees but on the nature of fees. We arbitrarily discussed that it would not be unforeseeable that fees could reach a $100 million per year amount considering the multi-disciplinary services being provided. Such amount did not trouble the participants as long as the nature of the services was not an issue." The Andersen accountants are effectively saying: "Although someone might think the level of our fees compromises our independence, in fact it does not, because it is the nature of those fees which is important—and therefore there are no ethical concerns, and we should carry on as before."

But this is to apply the wrong ethical standard. The correct standard, rather, concerns (b.) above: as we saw in Chapter 4, a practitioner should not undertake an engagement, if there would be even an appearance, to a reasonable observer, of compromised independence. And this concern is not similarly defeasible: if there simply appears to be a lack of independence (to a reasonable person), then, whether there is a lack of independence *in reality* is not relevant. So the distinction drawn between the 'level' and the 'nature' of fees was irrelevant. Andersen should have recognized—indeed, they apparently did recognize it, in the conference call—that there was an *appearance* of compromised independence, and this should have been sufficient to reach a judgment to disengage.

As we saw in Chapter 4, one reason why the mere appearance (to a reasonable observer) is decisive, is that we are poor judges in our own case. We are not suited, in our own case, to judge whether our judgment is really compromised, when it appears that it might be—precisely because, if it is compromised, we will lack the judgment to recognize that it is so. This would seem to be what happened with Andersen in relation to Enron. Andersen regarded itself as competent to decide that a reasonable claim of compromised judgment in fact had no substance. In hindsight we can see that that claim was correct, and that Andersen was wrong in dismissing it. And in hindsight we strongly suspect that it was precisely the unconscious, distorting motive of strong economic self-interest that had corrupted Andersen's judgment.

We saw in Chapter 4 that Independence was a necessary safeguard of Objectivity, and we distinguished Objectivity in thought from Objectivity in expression (or 'verbal Objectivity'). Objectivity in expression, we said, was equivalent to transparency: it implies making a representation of the financial condition of a company which is such that this representation naturally leads the intended audience to form a judgment about the company, which corresponds to the company's true condition. Andersen's lack of Objectivity in expression is also apparent in the internal memo. The memo states that, "A significant discussion was held regarding the related party transactions with LJM, including the materiality of such amounts to Enron's income statement and the amount retained 'off balance sheet'." If one considers this remark alone, one might think that Andersen had concluded that the debt concealed in the SPEs was so small as to be immaterial to a company the size of Enron. That judgment would not have been entirely unreasonable. But recall that Objectivity in expression implies thinking about the effect of one's representation on the intended audience. And in connection with this, a subsequent remark becomes telling: "We discussed Enron's reliance on its current credit rating to maintain itself as a high credit rated transaction party." That is to say, Andersen directly recognized that Enron's representations were sustaining a trust in the company, which was not however justifiable in substance. Enron's financial representations therefore lacked Objectivity in expression, yet Andersen continued to certify them.

Note that Enron's reluctance to disclose in its annual reports the details of SPE transactions, and the time and care it put into saying as little as possible about these, should have been a concern to Andersen, given its responsibility to the public interest. Indeed, Andersen should have been intent on clarifying for others precisely these obscure areas: "That impulse to avoid public exposure, coupled with the significance of the transactions for Enron's income statements and balance sheets, should have raised red flags for Senior Management, as well as for Enron's outside auditors and lawyers. Unfortunately, it apparently did not" (Powers Report, 201). Recall George Oliver May's remark from Chapter 4 that there is no room for 'weasel words' in anything to which an accountant gives a certificate.

Andersen, Integrity, and the Public Interest

We saw in Chapter 4 that Objectivity and a concern for Independence were 'virtues' of an accountant, which followed fairly directly from the 'distinctive work' of an accountant, involving service to the creditors and investors, actual or potential, in a company. This orientation of service is referred to as a concern for the Public Interest.

A concern for the Public Interest at first seems to be shown in the Watkins letter: "To the layman on the street, it will look like we recognized funds flow of $800mm from merchant asset sales in 1999 by selling to a vehicle (Condor) that we capitalized with a promise of Enron stock in later years....It sure looks to the layman on the street that we are hiding losses in a related company and will compensate that company with Enron stock in the future." And yet Watkins, although hailed as a 'whistle-blower', does not seem to rise to the level of a concern for the Public Interest. Her remarks seem more concerned with 'how it will look', and not so much with whether Enron's actions are harming others. For instance, later in the letter, where she puts forward possible scenarios for resolving the problem, she writes:

Develop clean up plan:

a. Best case: Clean up quietly if possible.

b. Worst case: Quantify, develop PR and IR campaigns, customer assistance plans (don't want to go the way of Salomon's trading shop), legal actions, severance actions, disclosure.

Watkins is an employee of Enron, but as a professional CPA, she has a responsibility to the Public Interest that transcends her employment there. It is not clear, however, that her concerns for her own standing ever rise to the level of professional integrity; they seem to be phrased more in terms of her career: "My 8 years of Enron work history will be worth nothing on my resume," she writes to Lay, "the business world will consider the past successes as nothing but an elaborate accounting hoax."

The point of these remarks is not to criticize Watkins, who showed undeniable candor in writing to Lay, and who in doing so certainly put her job at risk in the Enron culture, where notoriously 10% of staff were fired each year, regardless of performance. It is rather to establish a point of comparison. Watkins is universally regarded as the 'good guy' in the Enron scandal, rightly so, yet even her expressed remarks fall short of the standards expected of a CPA. (Note: this is an observation about her expressed remarks to Lay. Of course one cannot judge to what extent her own thoughts were different, and her way of describing the problem was dictated by 'tactical' considerations.)

In examining the Andersen memos, we do not even see the level of Watkins' concern for how the Enron SPEs would appear to an informed investor. As we saw, the memo very briefly mentions the materiality of

Enron's concealed debt. But its preoccupation is with Andersen and its interests, not the interest of the public. How much does the Enron engagement place Andersen at risk? What are the potential exposures? How much may nonetheless be gained from a continuing relationship? How much responsibility and therefore risk can be shifted to Enron or its Board of Directors? The Andersen memo displays not the slightest concern for the public interest.

In relation to this, think once more of McLean's piece in *Fortune*, and consider the sort of correction or restatement that Andersen was in February 2001 obliged to insist upon, given investors' reliance upon their audits. Not a single 'To Do' item coming out of the conference call had anything to do with Andersen's responsibility to the Public Interest.

Rules vs. Principles once again

Even the theme of Chapter 2 gets exhibited in the Enron scandal—that adherence to rules is not sufficient for propriety. This is clear from Andersen's handling of the Enron SPEs. The relevant accounting rule at the time stipulated that SPEs, to be truly independent, had to have at least 3% outside equity. But this is a necessary condition, not a sufficient condition of independence. *If an entity cannot be regarded as independent if it fails to have 3% equity, it does not follow that it will always be independent if it does have 3% equity.* The rule must be treated as a good starting point, which guides but does not substitute for professional judgment. By using good sense and good professional judgment—rather than merely being concerned to adhere to the rules—Andersen might have judged that the Enron SPEs were not truly independent and therefore, to avoid misrepresentation, had to be consolidated on the Enron balance sheet.

Note that, as the restatement acknowledged, Andersen in fact signed off on Enron SPEs where the outside equity was less than 3%. What this shows is that *when someone is not trying to follow the principle underlying the rule, then he won't even reliably follow the rule.* As we saw in Chapter 2, it is necessary to see rules as expressions or applications of principles, and to follow them in that spirit.

We used in chapter 2 the example of whether a lease should be treated as an operating or capital lease, for accounting purposes, as a good practical illustration of how rules are in the service of principles and should not trump principles. In particular, a lease in which ownership is in substance transferred should not be treated as an operating lease, even if there is some way of making the rules allow for that. Of course it was common in the pre-Enron era to do just that, in order to hide debt off-balance sheet—an analogue in its own way of Enron's more elaborate and pervasive use of SPEs. This practice of misrepresenting the substance of a lease arrangement took perhaps its most problematic form in the practice of "synthetic leases", in which one and the same transaction would be represented to the IRS as a purchase with incurred debt, for tax purposes, and as an operating lease, for financial reporting purposes. But it is not possible that one and the same lease arrangement be both: it is not possible that ownership be transferred and not transferred. If rules are in the service of principles, then the transaction gets recorded as it is, whatever the consequences for a company's financial report. Contrast with this Enron's practice of determining in advance what was expedient and then finding some way of making accounting rules allow for it—as in the Sherron Watkins quotation which we gave in chapter 1.

Andersen's treatment of Enron SPE's also verifies the maxim which we noted in Chapter 4, that good character and good culture require that one follow high standards of conduct in *small matters* and in *new circumstances*. People rightly wonder how Andersen could have arrived at the dismally corrupt outlook shown in its February 2001 memo, and even more so its actual destruction of documents later in the year, after the SEC had announced its intent to launch an investigation. But small indiscretions lead to large ones. Perhaps the fatal false step was Enron's use of an SPE in the early 1990s to move the liability of its Houston headquarters off-balance sheet. This arrangement had some color of justification then, but a conservative application of the principles underlying the construal of SPEs would have decided against it. Yet once this doubtful expedient was found to 'work', it was relied upon later, in more pressing circumstances, when Enron desperately needed to hide its mounting debt. Andersen could not later argue consistently against the device, without thereby implicitly judging itself to have been irresponsible in signing off on its use earlier. And by 2001 Andersen was eagerly cooperating with Enron to devise even more elaborate SPEs, effectively to cover for the failure of earlier ones. At every later step, it became more difficult and more costly to reverse course. Eventually Andersen took the reckless step of destroying Enron documents rather than admit its accumulating responsibility for the Enron fraud.

Illustrative legal case

We saw in *Feit v. Leisco* that the court regarded as settled fact that the Securities Acts were designed with the primary purpose of protecting the ordinary investor. In *U.S. v Arthur Young*, the Supreme Court attributed to accountants, consistent with professional standards and codes of conduct affirmed by accountants themselves, the public role as a kind of 'watchdog', in their work of auditing publicly traded companies. This role is additionally reinforced through the creation of the PCAOB, which was established by the following provision of Sarbanes-Oxley:

> There is established the Public Company Accounting Oversight Board, to oversee the audit of public companies that are subject to the securities laws, and related matters, in order to protect the interests of investors and further the public interest in the preparation of informative, accurate, and independent audit reports for companies the securities of which are sold to, and held by and for, public investors.

This provision in turn becomes the basis of the mission statement of PCAOB:

> The PCAOB is a private-sector, non-profit corporation, created by the Sarbanes-Oxley Act of 2002, to oversee the auditors of public companies in order to protect the interests of investors and further the public interest in the preparation of informative, fair, and independent audit reports.

Note the substitution of 'fair' for 'accurate', presumably to emphasize the importance of transparency in financial disclosures. Given that Sarbanes-Oxley makes PCAOB the highest authority as regards auditing standards for public accountants, it seems correct that the 'public watchdog' role articulated in *U.S. v. Arthur Young* is thereby given greater definiteness and reinforcement.

In light of these matters, it is striking to look at the dissenting opinion in *Bily v. Arthur Young* 834 P. 2d 745 (Cal 1992) , as indicating a certain tension in the law relative to the Code of Conduct accepted by accountants. *Bily* decided as regards California state law the scope of duty of care, and thus liability for negligence, for accountants as regards persons other than their clients. It did so by proposing a compromise as regards the three recognized standards: the traditional privity doctrine; the Restatement of Torts standard; and the Reasonable Foreseeability approach.[23] The California court held that each standard was relevant, depending upon the nature of an accountant's work and the degree of breach of the standard of care alleged: accountants have no general duty of care to anyone other than to their clients or restricted other parties as would be recognized under privity, for any work other than auditing; for negligent misrepresentations in an audit report, they are liable to the extent allowed under the more liberal Restatement approach; and finally, for misrepresentations in an audit report that amount to fraud, they are liable under the most expansive standard of the Reasonable Foreseeability approach.

The dissenting opinion in *Bily* argued that the expansive Reasonable Foreseeability standard should instead be used for negligent misrepresentation in an audit report. Here is a passage from its conclusion:

> The majority recognizes that accountants acknowledge a responsibility to third parties who foreseeably rely on audit reports in their business dealings with the audited company. Yet the majority adopts a rule that betrays the expectations of third party users whose reliance makes the audit report valuable to the audited company. Under the majority's rule, the audit report is made a trap for the unwary, because only the most legally sophisticated and well advised will understand that the report will not deliver what on its face it seems to promise: a qualified professional's actual assurance that the financial statement fairly states the financial situation of the audited company. An

---

[23] For a full discussion of the significance of these standards, see G. Spellmire, W. Baliga, and D. Winiarski, *Accounting, Auditing, and Financial Malpractice*, Harcourt Brace, 1998, pp. 11-26.

assurance with no legal recourse is essentially a hoax. Under the rule the majority adopts, any value that third parties place on the unqualified opinion is mistaken, because the law now insists that reliance upon the opinion, no matter how reasonable and foreseeable, is unjustified.

Finally, and perhaps most important, the majority pays too little attention to the importance of negligence liability as a means of preventing bad financial data from entering and polluting the waters of commerce. Without a liability rule that enforces the reasonable expectations of third party users of audit reports and provides an adequate incentive for due care, we may expect less careful audits, inefficient allocation of capital resources, increased transaction costs for loans and investments, and delay and disruption in the processes of lending and investing.

As in other opinions, as we have seen, we find first an argument based on the nature of the accountant's role, and then an argument appealing to consequences. The first argument is interesting because it effectively calls attention to the 'expectations gap', that is, the gap between what the ordinary investor thinks is certified by an unqualified audit report, and what the accounting profession commonly and appropriately regards itself to be certifying. The second argument, it would seem, has effectively been adopted by the U.S. Congress, since a similar line of thought underlies Sarbanes-Oxley and the formation of PCAOB.

The dissenting opinion in *Bily* highlights an apparent incongruence between the ethical standards accepted by accountants and the scope of liability allowed by the majority in that decision:

Because an accountant's moral, ethical, and professional responsibilities extend to foreseeable users of audit opinions, such as lenders and investors, an accountant whose carelessness causes economic loss to a foreseeable user is as morally blameworthy as an attorney who negligently drafts a will or contract, or a broker or escrow holder who negligently mishandles important documents in a real estate transaction. In each instance, the breach of a professional responsibility through lack of due care should result in liability to those to whom the professional owes an established moral and ethical obligation. Although defendant and the majority advance various arguments against this conclusion, none is persuasive.

The profession's standards propose a general responsibility to the public, but the majority recognizes an exposure to liability that falls short of that. Whatever the force of this consideration as a matter of law, one might expect that it would have weight at trial, before a jury. Members of a jury, one can suppose, would share in the same 'expectations gap' as the public at large and impute a correlative duty of care.

From this consideration, perhaps, the following important lesson can be gleaned, as an incidental conclusion: the argument that an accountant's liability in law should be more restricted than the extent of public reliance upon an accountant's work, can ultimately make sense only if there exist strong and demonstrably effective safeguards already in place, internal to the profession of accounting itself, so that legal protection of the investor's reasonable expectation becomes unnecessary. This, clearly, is what is referred to as the "obligation of self-discipline above and beyond the requirements of laws and regulations", inherent in the profession, to which we have many times referred.

One basic argument of this book has been: if this "obligation of self-discipline" is to have substance, then accountants must be principled and realize those principles in their work; and no accountant can succeed in acting in that way, unless he or she, individually, and corporately as a member of an esteemed profession, with the proper culture, is above all ethical.

Chapter 5 Review
Learning Objectives and Review Questions

Learning Objectives:

After reading this chapter you should be able to:
• Understand the nature and extent of the accounting improprieties in the Enron scandal.
• Identify specific lapses in integrity, independence, and objectivity in internal accounting and outside auditing at Enron.
• Understand how the Enron scandal clearly exemplifies the principles of accounting ethics and illustrates their indispensability.
• Construct a comparable analysis of other instances of accounting impropriety.
• View less dramatic lapses in accounting ethics as similar in substance to the Enron improprieties.

Questions for Review

1. When did Enron announce a restatement?
    a. February 6, 2001
    b. August 15, 2001
    c. November 8, 2001
    d. December 2, 2001
2. The Raptor SPEs were flawed because:
    a. They were controlled by an Enron employee.
    b. They were funded by Enron stock.
    c. They lacked 3% outside equity.
    d. All of the above.
3. Which of the following was not a reason offered by Bethany McLean in *Fortune* magazine for being skeptical of Enron's high stock price?
    a. The obscurity of Enron's business.
    b. Ethical doubts about Enron's management.
    c. Enron's high debt.
    d. Enron's low cash-flow.

4. Who said, "I wish we would get caught. We're such a crooked company."
  a. Sherron Watkins
  b. Andersen's Enron engagement officer
  c. An Enron manager
  d. An Andersen senior partner

5. Which of the following was not an explicit topic of the February 2001 Andersen conference call about its Enron engagement?
  a. Whether Andersen's Enron fees jeopardized its independence.
  b. Whether Andersen's Enron fees might reasonably appear to jeopardize its independence.
  c. Whether the nature of Andersen's Enron's fees did not jeopardize its independence.
  d. Whether the nature of Andersen's Enron's fees was a distinct matter from the amount of those fees.

6. Andersen's lack of concern for the Public Interest was shown in:
  a. Its lack of attention to obscurities in Enron's financial statements.
  b. Its focusing on Andersen's own exposure to risk and litigation.
  c. Its lack of attention to possible harms suffered by the investor.
  d. All of the above.

Consider the following passage from the March 21, 2002 oral testimony of Harvey Pitt, then Chairman of the SEC, before the Senate Committee on Banking, Housing and Urban Affairs, entitled "Accounting and Investor Protection Issues Raised by Enron and Other Public Companies'. (Lines are numbered for reference.)

1 It is also useful to recall that there were large audit failures long before accounting firms had any significant consulting business; merely mandating the separation of consulting from auditing — to create an "audit only" firm as some have suggested — does not guarantee an "audit failure free" future.

2 For one thing, an "audit only" firm also would be more dependent, not less, on their audit clients, and a single, large audit client could exert far

more influence on such a firm than is the case with firms that have multiple sources of revenues.

3 Moreover, information that can be gained through consulting engagements often is useful in performing audits....

4 Auditor independence is a dual-faceted problem.

5 Most importantly, those who perform the actual audits must be completely free of any pressures to waver from absolute and meticulous application of accounting principles.

6 When engagement partners are given additional compensation for cross-selling consulting services to the same client, they are exposed to the potential of divided loyalties.

7 We believe these practices need to be banned.

8 At the firm level, the critical goal should be to require and incentivize the firms to supervise and oversee the audit team, to make sure they perform audits not solely within the letter of auditing principles, but at the highest level of integrity.

9 One of the best ways to do this is to have a vigorous quality control review process, something the PAB [a proposed "Public Accountability Board", to become the PCAOB] we propose could do.

10 Each major firm should be reviewed by the PAB every year — not every three years — and be at risk to lose valued clients if their audits aren't deemed to be of top quality, whether or not they comply with minimum standards.

7. Consider Chairman Pitt's appeal to the notions of dependence and independence in lines 2 and 3. Which notion of independence does Pitt rely upon?

    a. Independence, the condition (see Chapter 4)

    b. Independence, the virtue (see Chapter 4)

    c. Both a. and b.

    d. A non-ethical notion of dependence, i.e. dependence upon information

8. Pitt appeals to the condition of Independence in which line?

    a. Line 3

    b. Line 5

    c. Line 8

    d. Line 10

9. In what line does Pitt rely on the main theme of Chapter 2, that compliance with rules is not sufficient for proper conduct?

    a. Line 1

    b. Line 2

    c. Line 6

    d. Line 8

10. Line 8, with its reference to incentives, supervision, and oversight, focuses especially on which notion from Chapter 4?

    a. Culture

    b. Professionalism

    c. Trust

    d. Public Interest

Suggested answers

1. c. Enron announced its restatement in November of 2001 and filed for bankruptcy within a month.

2. d. The Raptors and other Enron SPEs were flawed for all of the listed reasons. The Board of Directors voted an exception from the Enron Code of Ethics, allowing the Raptors to be controlled by Enron's own CFO; they were underwritten by Enron stock; and in fact they technically did not even satisfy the 3% rule.

3. b. The *Fortune* magazine piece was prescient but did not suspect how vast the fraud was at Enron.

4. c. Shockingly, this was said by an Enron manager familiar with the Raptor transactions.

5. b. And yet the appearance of a lack of independence was precisely the issue, because someone who looks to lack independence is not in a position to judge whether he in fact lacks independence.

6. d. Andersen recognized but did not correct the lack of transparency in the footnote of Enron annual report vaguely describing the Raptor arrangement; and they apparently put little weight on the risk carried by investors.

7.d. Dependence of X upon Y for information does not *ipso facto* imply a conflict of interest for X in dealings with Y or problems in maintaining objectivity.

8.b. If there are 'pressures to waver', then the condition of objectivity does not exist.

9.d. Pitt's phrase, 'not solely within the letter of auditing principles' is an example of the truth that compliance with rules is a necessary but not sufficient condition for propriety.

10.a. The general outlook of a firm supportive of scrupulously ethical accounting, as found in its incentives, supervision, and oversight, is the 'culture' of the firm.

WorldCom, a Failure in Professionalism and Integrity

IN WORLDCOM, AS IN ENRON, fraud was initiated at the highest levels of management. Accounting fraud was a result of this. At first, WorldCom may seem less egregious because, as we have seen, Andersen actively collaborated with Enron in designing its ultimately fraudulent use of off-balance sheet entities. External auditors in the WorldCom case, in contrast, were kept in the dark. Yet in WorldCom one sees a lapse in professional responsibility that, taken altogether, seems equally grave. How is it that Andersen was able to issue an unqualified audit report for WorldCom, when it was consistently denied access to the company's General Ledger? How is it that many CPAs internal to the company assisted management in committing fraud with very little protest or complaint? If Enron presents us with a failure of objectivity and independence, WorldCom shows an similarly serious failure in integrity and professionalism.

History of WorldCom and its business

"Bernie was out of his league", a telecom executive from the deep South commented after the precipitous fall of WorldCom. "He wasn't qualified to be the CEO of a global telecom company. You can try to spin it any way you want, but the bottom line is that he's a peddler. He likes to peddle and make deals...". The executive added:

> He didn't surround himself with good people to run the company. He personally couldn't do it. He was more intrigued with more mergers, more acquisitions, and more deals than he was with actually making money. They're just fortunate they experienced a period that we all did in our industry of 'crazy money,' that 1995-2000 time frame where even idiots could make money. You didn't have to outsmart the other guys. You didn't have to be that good. When that counted and mattered, people started falling left and right. WorldCom was no exception.[24]

This comment summarizes the nature of WorldCom's business and the key to its phenomenal growth. WorldCom was, so the speak, the breakup of AT&T but in reverse. In 1983, Judge Harold H. Greene ordered the breakup of AT&T, then the world's largest corporation. A condition of the breakup was that AT&T make available for lease its long-distance lines at substantial discounts. Entrepreneurs immediately saw the potential to make money quickly. Among these was a group of nine investors from Mississippi, including Bernie Ebbers, who started Long Distance Discount Services. Ebbers, with a net worth then of about $2 million from a hotel business, had formerly been employed as a milkman, bartender, bar bouncer, car salesman, truck driver, garment factory foreman, and high school basketball coach. Ebbers and the others were drawn to the argument of Murray Waldron, one of the original nine:

> If, for example, a customer could be charged $1 for a 50-cent phone call, and a simple piece of switching equipment required for routing the calls could handle 40 calls at once, the potential to make $20 a minute was extremely alluring. Using that example, if the switcher was maxed out around the clock, a phone company could make $28,800 a day, just for starters.[25]

---

[24] Lynne W. Jeter, *Disconnected: Deceit and Betrayal at WorldCom*, Hoboken, NJ: John Wiley & Sons, Inc., 2003, p. 161.
[25] Jeter, p. xxiv.

Of course other investors had the same idea, creating a competitive environment which pushed down prices. It became clear to Ebbers and his associates that success required that they quickly attain economies of scale. This required in turn the purchase of increasingly more expensive switching equipment, to provide service for large clients, such as business and public agencies. The strategy that eventually worked was acquisition and merger, underwritten by stock value after the company went public with the acquisition of Advantage Companies, a NASDAQ listed company, in 1989.

Deal-making was a great strength of Ebbers, who was elected CEO of LDDS in 1985. Ebbers put the company in the black and increased revenues to almost $100 million within three years:

> He had learned a very simple acquisition formula that guaranteed success. A reseller who was interested in selling to LDDS called the office and was faxed a short questionnaire, requesting a financial statement and a few other items. "We could look at it in no time and decide what we could pay," said a former LDDS accountant. "If his revenue was good and he was priced right, paying him six times annual revenues for his company was standard. The best he could get on his own was three or four multiples. We got to take, say, 12 times revenue off our next quarter's bottom line. It was a beautiful deal. And we found people like that all day long."[26]

Larger LDDS acquisitions in the early 1990s included Mid-American Communications, AmeriCall, FirstPhone, Advanced Telephone ($850 million), World Communications, Dial-Net, TRT, and Metromedia together with Resurgens ($1.25 billion). By now the company was called WorldCom and it was poised for truly phenomenal growth, with a series of major acquisitions and mergers:[27]

---

[26] Jeter, p. 42.

[27] Source: Robert S. Kaplan, David Kiron, "Accounting Fraud at WorldCom", Harvard Business School case study, 9-104-071, July 26, 2004.

1995	Williams Telecom	$2.5 billion
1996	MFS Communications TCL Telecom	$12.4 billion
1997	BLT Technologies NLnet	
1998	Brooks Fiber Properties CompuServe merger MCI	$2 billion $40 billion
1999	ActiveNet CAI Wireless Systems SkyTel	
2001	Intermedia Communications	$6 billion

WorldCom's growth came to an end with the sagging of the telecom industry, its loss of customers through the bursting of the dot.com bubble, and, perhaps most importantly, its failed merger with Sprint. "The kiboshing of the Sprint merger was, for all intents and purposes, the end of WorldCom," remarked accounting watchdog Howard J. Schilit, "When you have companies that have to make acquisitions to survive, once the music stops, the dance is over."[28]

In early 2002, WorldCom, with 60,000 employees, was reporting $30 billion in revenues and $104 billion in assets. But troubles were breaking out. In the wake of the failed Sprint merger, its stock price kept falling. In March, the SEC launched an investigation into alleged business improprieties. In May an article entitled, "Accounting for Anguish" appeared in the *Fort Worth Weekly* about Kim Emigh, who alleged that he was laid off from his job with WorldCom because he complained about shady financial practices, such as the company's decision in November 2001 not to pay vendors for the rest of the year, and the improper re-classification of labor in capital projects as an operating expense. The article included this prescient paragraph:

> The larger picture for WorldCom and MCI is that they are in a
> business that is in trouble and getting worse," said Pat Brogan, a

---

[28] Jeter, p. 120.

telecom analyst with the Precursor Group, an investor-side research firm. "The economics of the industry are miserable. The spotlight being shined on its accounting practices is putting a drag on the industry. A lot of the growth and hype that was surging the industry in the late '90s may have been fueled by accounting practices."[29]

Ebbers resigned as CEO in April 2002 and was succeeded by John Sidgmore. In early June, internal auditor Cynthia Cooper presented to the WorldCom audit committee evidence of widespread accounting fraud perpetrated by management. WorldCom stock dropped soon thereafter to pennies per share. Various state and federal criminal probes were launched. Finally, WorldCom filed for Chapter 11 bankruptcy protection on July 21, 2002. Many of its executives and several internal accountants were indicted. Its external auditor, Andersen, by that point had ceased to exist. On the Ides of March in 2005, Bernie Ebbers was convicted of securities fraud, conspiracy, and false filings. (As of the writing of this, he is awaiting sentencing.) The following day, the *Wall Street Journal* in its editorial pages opined that Ebbers' conviction might prove more salutary for corporate accounting than the entire apparatus of Sarbanes-Oxley regulation.

It was an astonishing spectacle—WorldCom's phenomenal rise and even faster fall, all within 20 years from the time that Ebbers and his friends put up $600,000 to start LDDS. That WorldCom's business would slow down was inevitable, and that its stock price had to sag was understandable. But that the company would crash and burn as it did, with substantial harm to investors and the nation's economy, was unnecessary, and purely the result of dishonesty, misrepresentation, and accounting malfeasance.

The nature of the fraud

WorldCom's fraud was designed to boost reported revenues in a depressed telecom market, so that the company might appear to satisfy a

---

[29] "Accounting for Anguish", by Gayle Reaves, *Fort Worth Weekly*, May 16, 2002, available at *Fort Worth Weekly Online*, http://www.fwweekly.com/issues/2002-05-16/feature.html /page1.html.

42% "line cost expenditure to revenue" (E/R) ratio set down as a criterion by industry analysts.

As we have seen, in the competitive telecom market of the late 1990s, companies such as WorldCom thrived by exploiting economies of scale that came from more extensive access to telecommunications lines through leasing—so-called "line costs".   This strategy of expansion worked well so long as demand was increasing.   Once demand fell, however, WorldCom and its competitors found themselves in a dilemma. On the one hand, they could not extricate themselves from these leases, which involved punitive termination fees.   On the other hand, industry analysts judged that the stock of a telecom company such as WorldCom would remain a good investment only so long as it maintained the E/R ratio that it showed in 2000, before the deterioration of the telecom market.

This was an industry-wide dilemma, not peculiar to WorldCom. It is important to stress this, because sometimes one might suppose that WorldCom's fraud constituted a harm principally against its own employees and investors in WorldCom stock. But the fraud was equally a harm against—because an unfair advantage relative to—the company's competitors, which for the most part faced the same difficulties as WorldCom, but which did not avail themselves of dishonest means. Admittedly, WorldCom was probably less able to deal with the difficulties than many of its competitors. Because it had acquired so many companies so quickly, it lacked good internal organization: it had to try to harmonize, for instance, dozens of different billing procedures and price plans. Furthermore, the main reason for its success never was good telecom business practice, but rather, as we have seen, a shrewd strategy of rolling up other companies.

The effort to maintain a 42% E/R ratio in a down market placed WorldCom employees at every level under tremendous pressure:

> WorldCom marketed itself as a high-growth company, and revenue growth was clearly a critical component of WorldCom's early success.   As market conditions throughout the telecommunications industry deteriorated in 2000 and 2001, WorldCom...nevertheless continued to post impressive revenue growth numbers, and Ebbers and [CFO Scott] Sullivan

continued to assure Wall Street that WorldCom could sustain that level of growth. In essence, WorldCom claimed it was successfully managing industry trends that were hurting all of its competitors. These promises of double-digit growth translated into pressure within WorldCom to achieve those results. As one officer told us, the emphasis on revenue was "in every brick in every building". [30]

This intense pressure to boost reported revenue would help to explain the dubious practices that Kim Emigh complained about. It also led WorldCom management and some employees to commit or be complicit in serious fraud.

WorldCom sustained its 42% E/R ratio through a series of fraudulent or questionable practices: the improper release of accruals (2Q 1999 through 2000); one time, top-side entries of undocumented revenue, recorded as "unallocated corporate" revenue (beginning 4Q 1999); a 'close the gap' approach to day-to-day accounting decisions (beginning 2Q of 2001-through 2002); and finally, and most audaciously, the capitalization of line costs (beginning 3Q 2000).

An accrual is revenue set aside to cover anticipated costs. WorldCom was typically billed months afterwards for leased lines that it was utilizing for business and revenue. Funds sufficient to make these payments would therefore be put aside in accrual accounts and counted toward line costs. It would be proper to release these funds, only if they were not needed to cover definite future expenses. From early 1999 until late 2000, at the direction of WorldCom CFO Sullivan and David Myers, the company Controller, approximately $3.3 billion was released improperly from accrual funds. Note that the effect of a release of accruals is to decrease line costs and to increase revenue correspondingly, thus shoring up the E/R ratio.

The improper releases of accruals had several features in common. They were directed by senior members of the corporate finance organization....They did not occur in the normal course of day-to-day operations, but instead in the weeks

---

[30] Dennis R. Beresford, Nicholas de B. Katzenbach, and C. B. Rogers, Jr., "Report of Investigation", Special Investigative Committee of the Board of Directors of WorldCom, Inc., March 31, 2003, p. 13.

following the end of the quarter in question. The timing and amounts of the releases were not supported by contemporaneous analysis or documentation. Most significantly, WorldCom employees involved in the releases generally understood at the time that they were improper. Some even raised concerns at the time of the releases.[31]

Even in the most complicated accounting frauds, it is usually possible to capture the essence of the fraud in a single phrase or sentence, because there are only a limited number of ways that one human being can cheat another. WorldCom's improper release of accruals was fraudulent, because it is impossible to use funds properly dedicated to line costs to 'pay down' line costs.

WorldCom's second fraudulent tactic lacked any finesse at all: increase the revenue of your company, simply by writing in numbers on your ledger as income:

Beginning in 1999, WorldCom personnel made large revenue accounting entries after the close of many quarters in order to report that it had achieved the high revenue targets that Ebbers and Sullivan had established....Most of the questionable revenue entries...were booked to "Corporate Unallocated" revenue accounts....The questionable revenue entries included in Corporate Unallocated often involved large, round-dollar revenue items (in millions or tens of millions of dollars). They generally appeared only in the quarter-ending month, and they were not recorded during the quarter, but instead in the weeks after the quarter had ended.[32]

Apparently WorldCom booked almost $2 billion of 'income' in this manner in 1999-2000. (If Ebbers had been able to make money like that in 1983, there would have been no need for all the trouble of starting a company.) Eventually Sullivan seems to have become concerned by how freely they were relying on this method to 'make the numbers', as evidenced in this voice message he left for Ebbers:

"Hey Bernie, it's Scott. This MonRev [monthly revenue report] just keeps getting worse and worse. The copy, um the latest

---

[31] Berensford, Katzenbach, and Rogers, p. 65.
[32] Berensford, Katzenbach, and Rogers, pp. 13-14.

> copy that you and I have already, has accounting fluff in it ...all
> one time stuff or junk that's already in the numbers. With the
> numbers being, you know, off as far as they were, I didn't think
> that this stuff was already in there...We are going to dig
> ourselves into a huge hole because year to date it's disguising
> what is going on on the recurring, uh, service side of the
> business...[33]

What Sullivan's message reveals is that, once they had resorted to lying
on a single occasion, it became easy for them to do so repeatedly, so that
they now actually had to rely on lying ("stuff or junk" in revenue
statements). It wasn't long before they were just as badly off, after the
lies were already factored in (the "stuff or junk" is "already in the
numbers"), than they were before, when they were not telling lies. Note
too that Sullivan apparently engages in the self-deceit that this
dishonesty is only a short-term matter, which they will eventually
compensate for: he refers to the unjustified entries as a 'hole' which,
presumably, they will eventually 'fill in' with legitimate income. Finally,
note Sullivan's concern that their reliance on deceit now makes it less
necessary for them to remedy the poor business practices which the
deceit was originally meant to compensate for. (When he refers to 'what
is going on, on the recurring, uh, service side of the business', he means
the telecom business!)

The third questionable accounting practice was referred to within
WorldCom as 'Close the Gap'. Here's how it worked:

> Throughout much of 2001, WorldCom's Business Operations
> and Revenue Accounting groups tracked the difference between
> projected and target revenue and kept a running tally of
> accounting "opportunities" that could be exploited to bridge
> that gap. What emerged was a coordinated and institutionalized
> process in which revenue "opportunities" were identified,
> measured and booked in the amount needed to hit the
> Company's external growth projections.[34]

This is an excellent example of the manipulation and exploitation of
accounting rules in order to represent a company's condition in the way

---

[33] Berensford, Katzenbach, and Rogers, p. 15.
[34] Berensford, Katzenbach, and Rogers, p. 14.

that the management wants it to be represented, regardless of whether this gives a fair or true picture ('form over substance'), rather than letting principles control the use of accounting rules, so that those rules serve as constraints and correctives ('substance over form'). The result is determined not with a view to truthfulness and fair presentation, but with a view to targets and interests set from the outside. The "Close the Gap" program seems to have been responsible for constructing about a billion dollars of questionable revenue.

The fourth and most egregious accounting malfeasance at WorldCom, however, was its shift in 2001 to capitalizing line costs. We saw in chapter 2 above that a lease can sometimes be treated as an operating expense and sometimes as an expenditure on capital. There are close calls, and the relevant principle is, roughly, that a lease can be capitalized if, in leasing the item, one assumes in substance the benefits, risks, and burdens of ownership. The lease of a telecommunications line is clearly not like that, and therefore it must be treated as an operating expense, as indeed all telecom companies besides WorldCom were doing, and as WorldCom itself was doing, until, curiously enough, faced with extreme business pressures—and all accrual accounts had been depleted!—Sullivan and Ebbers came to the realization that a different accounting treatment would then be warranted.

Of course it would be very *favorable* to WorldCom if line costs could reasonably be capitalized: this would have the effect of decreasing line costs (which are operating expenses) and therefore the E/R ratio, and, correspondingly, increasing the company's assets. How extensive was WorldCom's reliance on this hoax? The Table 6-1 below from the SEC complaint against two of the accountants who made the illicit entries tells the tale.

Call a 'distinterested judgment' a decision we reach when there are no reasons of self-interest to decide one way or another. Call an 'interested judgment' a decision we reach, when there are pressures or incentives to decide in a certain way, and we happen to decide in the way that matches our self-interest. In July 2000, an internal accountant for WorldCom, Tony Minert, CPA, who had been given the task of looking into the reduction of line costs, floated a proposal to Sullivan and Myers:

I have been making some phone calls trying to find out why our cost[s] are increasing for this quarter and from what I am gathering it sounds like we are starting to get a network out there that has a lot of extra capacity...If we could somehow take that...underutilized network...into an[] inventory or prepaid account and only booked it as expense when we have the revenue to match it, then this might help with our e/r numbers. I would think that our cost would be at a 42% e/r. ...I am definitely going to go down this alley because this would help out our cause tremendously, and I have got to think that there is something we could do.[35]

In July 2000 accrual accounts had not yet been depleted, and "Corporate Unallocated" revenues were working well enough. In these circumstances, where there were yet no self-interested reasons for deciding one way or another, Myers and Yates considered Minert's idea of capitalizing the network's unused capacity and, rendering a disinterested judgment, quickly rejected it as unsupportable under GAAP. After Minert raised the issue several more times in July, Yates wrote to Myers: "David, I might be narrow minded, but I can't see a logical path for capitalizing excess capacity. Your thoughts?" Myers agreed. Yates informed Minert that his idea had no accounting support: "Tony, David [Myers] and I have reviewed and discussed your logic of capitalizing excess capacity and can find no support within current accounting guidelines that would allow for this accounting treatment."

However, within a few months Scott Sullivan had decided that line costs for underutilized lines *should* be capitalized, and he directed that entries be made accordingly, in the amounts listed in Table 6-1. That Sullivan's judgment was 'interested' and not made in good faith is clear for five reasons.[36]

1. Sullivan had no plausible argument for that change in accounting treatment. When the fraud was discovered in the summer of 2002 by Cynthia Cooper, and the WorldCom Audit Committee asked Sullivan to give a justification, the two-page "White Paper" that he wrote for them

---

[35] Berensford, Katzenbach, and Rogers, p. 98.
[36] Ibid.

explaining the practice was entirely ad hoc, citing irrelevant accounting rules, and containing no remotely plausible arguments.

2. The adjustments to line costs and balance sheets mandated by Sullivan bore no relation to actual underutilized capacity but were exactly what was needed to meet the 42% E/R criterion.

3. The capitalizations were not placed in their proper categories but distributed randomly throughout the balance sheet, as if to hide the fact.

4. Sullivan never discussed the change of accounting treatment with the external auditors, as would be usual with a judgment call made in good faith.

5. If the accounting change had been introduced in good faith, then presumably it would have been disclosed openly in public filings, but it wasn't.

TABLE 6-1: WorldCom's False Statements in Filings with the SEC Third Quarter 2000 Through First Quarter 2002 [37]

Form Filed With the Commission	Reported Line Cost Expenses	Actual Line Cost Expenses	Reported Income before Taxes and Minority Interests	Actual Income (Loss) before Taxes and Minority Interests
10-Q, 3rd Qtr 2000	$3.867 billion	$4.695 billion	$1.736 billion	$908 million
10-K, 2000	$15.462 billion	$16.697 billion	$7.568 billion	$6.333 billion
10-Q, 1st Qtr 2001	$4.108 billion	$4.879 billion	$988 million	$217 million
10-Q, 2nd Qtr 2001	$3.73 billion	$4.29 billion	$159 million	($401 million)
10-Q, 3rd Qtr 2001	$3.745 billion	$4.488 billion	$845 million	$102 million
10-K, 2001	$14.739 billion	$17.754 billion	$2.393 billion	($622 million)
10-Q, 1st Qtr 2002	$3.479 billion	$4.297 billion	$240 million	($578 million)

---

[37] United States District Court for the Southern District of New York 02 CV 8083 (JSR) COMPLAINT (Securities Fraud) Securities and Exchange Commission, Plaintiff, v. BETTY L. VINSON, and TROY M. NORMAND, Defendants.

Now people usually do not act dishonestly unless there is some patina of justification, some stretch of a plausible argument, that rationalizes what they are doing. The capitalization of line costs, which as if by magic converts an expense into an asset, looks so ludicrous, that one wonders how it might in any way have appeared justifiable. We suggest that an underlying fallacy was at work. Recall once again that a lease can be capitalized if, through the lease, one assumes the burdens and risks of ownership. WorldCom was certainly burdened by the transmission lines it had leased but was not utilizing. And one might feel that the burden was *analogous* at least to the burden of an asset that one purchases for use on a future date: for instance, I purchase in the summer a snow blower that is on sale at a good price, since I anticipate using it in the winter, and in the meantime I have the burden of owning it (I assume the costs of storage, insurance, depreciation, and so on). But the analogy fails, because a burden devolved upon WorldCom not because of the leased lines, but because of their (poor, overly optimistic) decision to lease the lines in advance of demand. Suppose I buy 10 snow-blowers, because I expect a hard winter, and I want to start a small snow-removal business, but it turns out to be a mild winter, and I can make use of only one. Then I have two distinct burdens: (i) the burden of storing and insuring, etc., so many snow blowers, and (ii) the 'burden' on my resources of having committed (as it turns out mistakenly) so much capital to acquiring snow-blowers. The second burden is a consequence of judgment, not ownership, and that is the sort of burden that WorldCom had to bear in connection with unused lines. It is a fallacy to mistake that for the burden of ownership.

But one might wonder still about the entire policy of fraud adopted by WorldCom's executives. Couldn't they see that they were being dishonest, through and through? And how could they dare to do what they did, if they saw it squarely as fraudulent? But we may speculate that they thought their desperate steps were for a good cause. In the preceding chapter, we noted that Enron had the characteristics of a Ponzi scheme: Enron's core businesses in the 1990s became unimportant compared with its energy futures trading. That business, because of its success, fostered unrealistic investor confidence and resulted in Ponzi-like structures and incentives. In a Ponzi scheme, there is no real business, and income derives rather from growth, that is, from signing on new customers, who pay in advance in expectation of a service or return. A Ponzi scheme by its nature requires growth; it cannot sustain itself in the absence of growth. Moreover, we saw that, in such an arrangement, the very *expectation* of growth ends up being essential to growth. *The fostering of that expectation becomes essential to the business.* Enron was like that, which helps to explain why, in such circumstances, its management might have come to think of fraud as a positive good. Fraud (it can appear) will actually *benefit* employees and investors, on the grounds that it preserves the *expectation* of success that is essential to the perception of the company's success. Moreover, management can successfully fool itself that the fraud is only a temporary expedient, useful for getting a company through a slow period, until the company can resume once more its successful strategy of growth.

WorldCom, because its explosive growth came from mergers and acquisitions, not from its core business, similarly developed something of a Ponzi-structure. Its continued success depended upon continued expansion; but that depended upon acquisitions; but that required a strong stock price; but that in turn required the expectation of continued success. "It seems clear that WorldCom's ability to borrow monies was facilitated by its massive accounting fraud," according to Richard Thornburgh, "which allowed the Company to falsely present itself as creditworthy and 'investment grade'. It also seems clear that the Company's ability to borrow vast sums allowed it to perpetuate the illusion of financial health created by its accounting fraud."[38] In these circumstances, it would be natural for WorldCom management, then, when faced with what, for all they knew, was a brief downturn in the telecom market, to try to prop up or puff up expectations, until the market strengthened and the company could resume its earlier pattern of success. Fraud would appear an unpleasant expedient, necessary only for the short-term, which in the long run would benefit thousands of employees and millions of investors, not to mention the local economy.

Ebbers presented a substantially false picture to the market, to the Board of Directors, and to most of the Company's own

---

[38] Statement of Dick Thornburgh, WorldCom Bankruptcy Examiner, Before the Senate Committee on the Judiciary, Tuesday, July 22, 2003.

employees. At the same time he was projecting, and then reporting, continued vigorous growth, he was receiving internal information that was increasingly inconsistent with those projections and reports. Moreover, he did not disclose the persistent use of non-recurring items to boost reported revenues. Ebbers was aware, at a minimum, that WorldCom was meeting revenue expectations through financial gimmickry. Yet he kept making unrealistic promises, and failed to disclose the existence of these devices or their magnitude.[39]

The failure of the accountants

One sees a kind of fool's parade of accounting tricks carried out by WorldCom management over a period of roughly three years, and this in circumstances which should have prompted suspicion, since it was puzzling that WorldCom should continue to achieve double-digit revenue growth, when all the other telecoms were barely avoiding losses. What role did accountants play in this? Why did internal auditors fail to detect the fraud? Why were internal accountants complicit? How did a fraud of this magnitude, and which lacked the complexity of Enron's SPEs, escape detection by Andersen, WorldCom's external auditors? We might speculate that not a few internal accountants in WorldCom were aware of the disparity between Ebbers' representations to the market and the internal picture of the company. How did they understand their own role as regards these misrepresentations?

The WorldCom scandal was made possible because some accountants failed to live the virtues of accountancy, and failed to adhere to the principles and ideals of their profession. Worse than this: Ebbers, Sullivan, and Myers presumed that it would be so. Even in a post-Enron environment, they acted on the presumption that the accountants whose cooperation they needed to perpetrate their fraud would not oppose them (at the price of losing their jobs), or would turn a blind eye, or would even assist them—and, sad to say, they were proved right in this. Let us consider in turn the internal accountants, external auditors, and internal auditors of WorldCom.

---

[39] Berensford, Katzenbach, and Rogers, p. 21.

The complicity of internal accountants

But how *should* internal accountants have acted at WorldCom? The answer, as we have seen from chapter 4 above, is that they should have refused from the start to cooperate with accounting practices that had even the appearance of deceit or impropriety, even if this implied the loss of their jobs—just as we expect policemen, firefighters or physicians to carry out their professional obligations even if that implies personal risk. They should have been prepared to do so as a 'united front', so that it would have seemed hopeless to Sullivan or Ebbers that they could ever induce members of the accounting profession to 'budge' from the highest standards.

A good example of that kind of professionalism is how the physicians of Holland acted under the Nazi occupation in World War II. Their heroic stance is described in a classic study of the failure of professionalism in German medicine, Dr. Leo Alexander's "Medicine Under Dictatorship", first published in the *New England Journal of Medicine*, July 14, 1949, pp. 39-47. Dr. Alexander writes:

> There is no doubt that in Germany itself the first and most effective step of propaganda within the medical profession was the propaganda barrage against the useless, incurably sick... Similar, even more subtle efforts were made in some of the occupied countries. It is to the everlasting honor of the medical profession of Holland that they recognized the earliest and most subtle phases of this attempt and rejected it. When Sciss-Inquart, Reich Commissar for the Occupied Netherlands Territories, wanted to draw the Dutch physicians into the orbit of the activities of the German medical profession, he did not tell them "You must send your chronic patients to death factories" or "You must give lethal injections at Government request in your offices," but he couched his order in most careful and superficially acceptable terms. One of the paragraphs in the order of the Reich Commissar of the Netherlands Territories concerning the Netherlands doctors of 19 December 1941 reads as follows: "It is the duty of the doctor, through advice and effort, conscientiously and to his best ability, to assist as helper

the person entrusted to his care in the maintenance, improvement and re-establishment of his vitality, physical efficiency and health. The accomplishment of this duty is a public task." The physicians of Holland rejected this order unanimously because they saw what it actually meant—namely, the concentration of their efforts on mere rehabilitation of the sick for useful labor, and abolition of medical secrecy. Although on the surface the new order appeared not too grossly unacceptable, the Dutch physicians decided that it is the first, although slight, step away from principle that is the most important one. The Dutch physicians declared that they would not obey this order. When Sciss-Inquart threatened them with revocation of their licenses, they returned their licenses, removed their shingles and, while seeing their own patients secretly, no longer wrote death or birth certificates. Sciss-Inquart retraced his steps and tried to cajole them—still to no effect. Then he arrested 100 Dutch physicians and sent them to concentration camps. The medical profession remained adamant and quietly took care of their widows and orphans, but would not give in. Thus it came about that not a single euthanasia or non-therapeutic sterilization was recommended or participated in by any Dutch physician. They had the foresight to resist before the first step was taken, and they acted unanimously and won out in the end. It is obvious that if the medical profession of a small nation under the conqueror's heel could resist so effectively, the German medical profession could likewise have resisted had they not taken the fatal first step. It is the first seemingly innocent step away from principle that frequently decides a career of crime. Corrosion begins in microscopic proportions.

The Dutch physicians, and their shrewd resistance to subterfuge, even to the point of death, serve as an example of professionalism at its best. In this connection, it is important to recognize that fraud at WorldCom was carried out with the assistance of many accountants. And one might reasonably presume that, for these accountants likewise, the first, small step of compromise was the fatal step:

Awareness of this financial fraud was not confined to just two or three people. Others at WorldCom either knew or suspected that senior financial management was engaged in improper accounting. These included not only people in the General Accounting group...who ordered or implemented the entries, but people in other financial reporting and accounting groups whose responsibilities were affected by them. Employees in several such groups suggested, made or knew of entries that were not supportable, or prepared reports that were false or misleading as a consequence. Remarkably these employees frequently did not raise any objections despite their awareness or suspicions that the accounting was wrong, and simply followed directions or even enlisted the assistance of others. Some of them complained to their supervisors or, in a handful of cases, refused to take actions they considered inappropriate. However, none took effective action to try to halt or expose these practices until the Spring of 2002. Employees in the financial and accounting groups believed that forcefully objecting to conduct that they knew was being directed by Sullivan would cost them their jobs; few of them were prepared to take that risk.[40]

Admittedly, because of the Byzantine organizational structure of WorldCom, it was possible for supervisors to deflect concerns about undocumented entries.

More than one employee described WorldCom as a series of isolated "silos" where each group knew and understood its own costs and revenues but had no knowledge about other groups and never shared information with the others. When employees raised concerns about reductions of their accruals or other apparent misconduct, senior management could always—and frequently did—say that the issue was resolved and acceptable at the consolidated, total company level.[41]

And Ebbers and Sullivan no doubt benefited, too, from the principle of the 'big lie', namely, if a lie is outlandish enough, no one will believe that

---

[40] Berensford, Katzenbach, and Rogers, p. 7.
[41] Berensford, Katzenbach, and Rogers, p. 20.

you are lying, because it would seem too easy for the lie to be found out. Yet, on the whole, WorldCom accountants were 'simply following orders', so to speak, and they did what they were told, not even bothering to consider whether what they were asked to do met standards of truthfulness and integrity: "Many, even those with accounting degrees and CPA designations, told us that they viewed their job as simply entering numbers."[42]

People usually need to employ euphemisms to hide misconduct from themselves. For instance, as mentioned, there was a ripple effect from the imposition by highest management of the capitalized line costs: "The accounting entries necessary to shift line costs to capital accounts were relatively simple for the General Accounting group to make, but they had ripple effects in other areas of the Company". Property Accounting, in charge of expenditures, and Capital Reporting, responsible for tracking assets, had to reconcile their books as regards these "capital assets" that unaccountably were added to their inventory, as they did for authorized and reported acquisitions. They euphemistically referred to these dubious adjustments as "non cash adjustments": "Employees in those two groups described regular conversations about the capitalization entries, which they called "non-cash adjustments."[43]

The failure of the external auditor

Andersen as the external auditor apparently failed as regards independence and due-diligence. It might be thought that the latter followed from the former.

Andersen's doubtful independence is evident in language the firm used to describe its relationship to WorldCom.

Andersen told the [WorldCom] Audit Committee in its Year 2000 Audit Proposal that it understood the business issues and risks associated with WorldCom's operations, and that it considered itself "a committed member of [WorldCom's] team."

...Indeed, in a presentation to the Audit Committee on May 20,

---

[42]Ibid.

[43] Berensford, Katzenbach, and Rogers, p. 104.

1999, Andersen stated that it viewed its relationship with WorldCom as a "long-term partnership", in which Andersen would help WorldCom improve its business operations and grow in the future. [44]

Needless to say, "partnership" and "team member" are phrases suggestive of an advocacy or collaborative role, and are inappropriate to the position of an independent auditor, which has a responsibility to render objective judgment in the service of the public interest. This language and outlook was mirrored in the close business relationship of Andersen with WorldCom: from 1999 to 2000 WorldCom paid Andersen $7.8 in audit fees but about $50 million for other services, including tax services and consulting.

In its presentations to the WorldCom Audit Committee, Andersen stated explicitly that it would not use a "traditional audit approach" which would involve verifying the information on accounting records and financial statements, and a focus on account balances. Rather, Andersen told the Audit Committee that it would provide a new kind of audit, a "controls-based" or "risk-based" approach. Such an approach depends heavily on internal controls, the reliability of which is the responsibility of management. In fact Andersen requested from management the same 20 to 30 schedules each quarter, a predictability which would make its work especially vulnerable to manipulation by management.

Andersen failed to cultivate an appropriate attitude of skepticism about WorldCom management. They used software which gave the result that WorldCom was only a 'high' risk client. Andersen partners overrode this result and rated WorldCom as 'maximum' risk. Yet then Andersen failed to take the steps that the firm required for maximum risk clients, and they failed to inform the Audit Committee that they regarded WorldCom in this light. In their audit of the highly relevant area of capital expenditure,

> Andersen's auditing methodology was in large part premised on the assumption that capital expenditures would arise through proper means—specific capital projects that could be tracked—and, based on the work papers, does not appear to have

---

[44] Berensford, Katzenbach, and Rogers, p. 223-4.

implemented any procedures to address the possibility that they would be created through accounting fraud.[45]

In a June 2001 "fraud brainstorming" session, Andersen auditors met to discuss possible problem areas regarding WorldCom. They specifically identified improper capitalization and top-side adjustments as issues to be concerned about for WorldCom. Yet the firm apparently took no special steps to test these areas.

Andersen repeatedly asked to be able to examine the General Ledger of the company, and their request was uniformly denied. Of course, if they were able to examine the General Ledger, they would likely have quickly discovered the sizeable, whole number top-side entries. They should not have issued an unqualified audit report on WorldCom without access to the General Ledger.

Andersen also overlooked tips and clues which, if interpreted with an appropriate concern over fraud, might conceivably had led them to detect the WorldCom accounting irregularities. For instance, in October 2000 a WorldCom employee told Andersen UK that, over his protestations, he was required by a US WorldCom office to release, without documentation or explanation, an accrual to the amount of $33.6 million dollars, as a result of which he regarded himself as underaccrued. Andersen UK reported the matter to Andersen's WorldCom engagement team, which apparently failed to follow up on the matter, having accepted a WorldCom executive's cursory explanation as satisfactory.

The internal auditor

Internal Auditing at WorldCom reported directly to Scott Sullivan, the mastermind of the frauds, and thus we may suspect, as was indeed the case, that their activities were directed by Sullivan in such a way as to keep them from discovering anything that might alert them to the fraud. And because they reported directly to Sullivan, employees who saw something doubtful or suspicious would be reluctant to approach them.

Internal Audit is the closest thing to a hero in the WorldCom decline. The story was told in major media, and Cynthia Cooper, head of internal audit, became something of a celebrity, even being named a

---

[45] Berensford, Katzenbach, and Rogers, p. 225.

Time Magazine Person of the Year for 2002. Cooper and some colleagues in May and June of 2002 pressed forward with an audit of Capital Expenditures, downloading data late at night to avoid raising suspicions. Once they gained access to the General Ledger, they quickly identified the large, round number capitalization entries. When they approached Myers about them, who said he could give no justification, they went to the Audit Committee, and that is how the WorldCom fraud came to light.

And yet even Internal Audit is not an unblemished hero. Internal Audit had commenced a Capital Expenditures Audit the preceding year, in December 2001. In the course of the audit, they sought information from Capital Reporting. The employees there, who knew all about "non-cash adjustments", were unsure what to do. Should they include these adjustments in what they sent to Internal Audit or not? (Needless to say, they should not have hesitated to inform Internal Audit about them.) By some fluke or mistake, the "non-cash adjustments" were included. These totaled $2.3 billion dollars, under the heading 'Corporate'! (Compare: during the same time period, WorldCom's entire expenditures on telecommunications equipment was only slightly more, at $2.9 billion.) Internal Audit asked for an explanation ("Just so I have an answer," an Internal Audit Manager wrote, "What kinds of projects make up the bulk of Corporate?"); apparently what they heard satisfied them; and in their final report the $2.3 billion is simply omitted. Thus Internal Audit failed to follow up on a big clue that, by some fluke, was placed directly in their path.

Conclusion

If Enron, with its complicated system of SPEs, is a failure in ethics of accountants working at a very high level of technical expertise—'the smartest guys in the room'—WorldCom provides a sobering example of how massive fraud may be perpetrated when ordinary practitioners lose sight of professionalism, and of the sacrifice of self-interest that true professionalism sometimes requires, and instead excuse their own complicity in fraud on the grounds that they were 'following the rules.'

Chapter 6 Review
Learning Objectives and Questions for Review

Learning Objectives:

After reading this chapter you should be able to:
• Give an overview of WorldCom's history and business.
• Explain the extent and nature of fraud at WorldCom.
• Identify shortcomings in internal accounting at WorldCom.
• Identify shortcomings in Andersen's approach to WorldCom.
• Draw lessons of professionalism from the WorldCom example.

Questions for Review

1. What was the original name of the company that eventually became WorldCom?
    a. The Phone Company.
    b. ADHD
    c. LDDS.
    d. MCI.

2. Which of the following jobs did Bernie Ebbers not hold before becoming CEO in the company that was to become WorldCom?
    a. hotelier
    b. phone technician
    c. bartender
    d. milkman

3. A line cost is:
    a. A deduction from the bottom line.
    b. The cost of installing a telephone line.
    c. The cost of leasing a telephone line.
    d. The straight line depreciation cost of telephone switching equipment.

4. What event effectively brought an end to WorldCom's expansion?
    a. Its merger with MCI.

b. The failed Sprint merger.

c. Declaration of bankruptcy in 2002.

d. Ebbers' resignation as CEO.

5. What is the E/R ratio?

    a. earnings to risk

    b. expenditure to revenue

    c. excess capacity to reserve capacity

    d. extra service to referral service

6. Which of the following accounting irregularities did WorldCom not use?

    a. SPEs

    b. improper release of accruals

    c. capitalization of operating expenses

    d. unsupported top-side adjustments

7. What word did Scott Sullivan not use to refer to top-side adjustments as reflected in monthly revenue reports?

    a. stuff

    b. junk

    c. fluff

    d. padding

8. What was the name of WorldCom's institutionalized bending of accounting rules to reach target revenue figures?

    a. Mind the Gap

    b. Close the Gap

    c. Think Straight, Talk Straight

    d. Team Accounting

9. Which of the following does improper release of accruals not achieve?

    a. reduced line costs

    b. increased revenue

    c. lower E/R ratio

    d. increased assets

10. Which of the following is not a reason why Sullivan did not capitalize line costs in good faith?

    a. Capitalizations were unrelated to unused capacity.

    b. Capitalizations were not placed in proper categories.

    c. Capitalizations were never disclosed.

    d. Capitalizations were discussed with Andersen.

11. Which class of professionals acted in an entirely exemplary fashion as regards WorldCom?

    a. internal auditors

    b. internal accountants

    c. external auditors

    d. none of the above

12. In a "fraud brainstorming" session, Andersen identified which of the following as risks for WorldCom:

    a. improper capitalization

    b. SPEs

    c. 'round-trip' transactions

    d. cookie-jar reserves

Suggested answers:

1. c.

2. b.

3. c. Early regional long-distance companies leased long distance lines at a discounted rates and then resold.

4. b.

5. b.

6. a. SPEs were not important in the WorldCom fraud. WorldCom accounting irregularities were relatively simple to understand.

7. d.

8. b.

9. d. Accruals have no effect on the balance sheet, since they are revenues set aside for an anticipated liability.

10 d. No WorldCom official discussed the idea of capitalizing line costs with Andersen, as one would normally do for a major change in accounting treatment proposed in good faith.

11. d. Even the internal auditors seemed to drop the ball, in their December 2001 Capital Expenditure audit.

12. a. Although it identified this, Andersen apparently never tried to take special steps to insure it wasn't happening.

Can Accounting Ethics Be Taught?

IT IS OFTEN CLAIMED that ethics cannot be taught. If so, the study of accounting ethics, or of any other sort of professional ethics, would be futile and a waste of time. So this concern needs to be addressed. Can accounting ethics be taught?

We believe that it can. But doubts about this, which are reasonable, should be diffused. In this chapter, then, we first give the other side the fullest possible say, formulating ten reasons why someone might think that ethics cannot be taught. Then in reply, and drawing on what we have already considered in previous chapters, we will show that these contrary arguments are mistaken. In fact, ethics can be taught, and we will clarify exactly how.

Ethics, even ethics as applied to the professions, is properly a branch of philosophy. But the correct method in philosophy involves not simply showing why the right view is true, but also showing why incorrect views, although reasonable and well motivated, are false. A philosophical difficulty always needs to be dissolved as well as solved.

Our first step will be to begin with the proper context. We claimed in chapter 3 above that classical philosophy provides the best framework for accounting ethics. Yet classical philosophers were the first to pose, and answer, this question of whether ethics can be taught. It turns out, then, that the best entry into the subject is to consider how classical philosophers approached the question—to which we now turn.

An ancient problem

"It's possible to teach about ethics, to be sure, but can we teach ethics? We can teach what ethical accounting is, but can we teach accountants to be ethical?" These questions are variations of what is in fact an ancient concern, dating back to the Greek philosophers, Socrates, Plato, and Aristotle.

Socrates (469-399 B.C.) lived in Athens and devoted his life to exhorting his fellow citizens to live virtuously. He was eventually put on trial, on charges of putatively 'corrupting young people and denying the religion of the state', but probably in fact because his incessant questioning humiliated and angered many prominent Athenians. Socrates explained his understanding of his own life and mission in the following way during his trial:

> If you say to me, 'Socrates, this time we ... will let you off, but on one condition only—that you stop inquiring and speculating in this way, and that, if you were to be caught doing this again, you would be put to death.' If this were the condition on which you were to let me go, I should reply: 'Men of Athens, I honor and love you. But I shall obey God rather than you. And while I have life and strength I shall never cease practicing and teaching philosophy, exhorting in my usual manner anyone whom I meet, and persuading him, saying: 'O my friend, why do you—a citizen of the great and mighty and wise city of Athens—care so much about accumulating the greatest amount of money and honor and reputation, and so little about wisdom and truth and the greatest improvement of the soul, which you never pay any attention to at all? Are you not ashamed of this?' And if the person I engage in this way says: 'But I do care about these things!', I don't walk away, and I don't let him leave. Rather, I interrogate him, and I examine and cross-examine him. And if I think that he lacks virtue—that he is only claiming that he has virtue—I reproach him with undervaluing the greater, and overvaluing the less (Plato's *Apology*).

He reproaches his fellow citizens with valuing only 'instrumental goods', as we have called them, and not those goods that, we saw, are and should be regarded as incommensurably higher.

It was a noble defense speech, but not calculated to be effective with the jury. The majority of the jury apparently took Socrates to be obnoxiously boastful and arrogant and sentenced him to death.

Socrates' gifted follower, Plato, was watching on as his teacher was arrested, put on trial, and put to death. He saw Socrates devote all his energies to encouraging his fellow Athenians to be virtuous, but the end result was that Socrates was crushed, and unprincipled people apparently triumphed. Naturally enough, Plato questioned the basic premise of Socrates' life. Was it all futile? Was Socrates perhaps mistaken in presuming, as he apparently did, that virtue can be taught? This is the question with which Plato begins his famous dialogue, the *Meno*, when the chief character, Meno, asks the fictional Socrates the following question:

Can you tell me, Socrates, whether virtue is acquired by teaching or by practice; or if neither by teaching nor practice, then whether it comes to man by nature, or in what other way?

Plato's tentative answer, later in the dialogue, consists of a hypothetical: if virtue is a kind of knowledge, then it can be taught—because knowledge is the sort of thing that can be imparted to others.

But is virtue in fact a kind of knowledge? Plato had his doubts. He pointed out that there are no recognized experts in virtue in society, yet there are recognized experts for various sorts of knowledge. There is medical knowledge, and physicians are recognized experts in that sort of knowledge. There is knowledge of construction, and builders are recognized experts in that. There is knowledge of caring for horses, and horse-trainers are recognized experts in that. But if there were some sort of knowledge involved in being a good human being, then there ought to be recognized experts in human goodness. But, Plato thought, there don't seem to be such experts.

Plato also pointed out that the leaders of Athens who were generally regarded as extremely virtuous—men such as Themistocles and Pericles—typically had children who were not virtuous. It was striking that the children of these men did learn horse riding and military skill and musical skill from their father, but they did not learn how to be virtuous. However, Plato argued, surely a father would be more concerned about imparting this to his child than those other skills. The fact that fathers did not, after all, succeed in imparting virtue to their children, then, was a sign that virtue could not be thus imparted—that it wasn't some kind of expertise or knowledge.

Aristotle, who was Plato's student, did not share his teacher's worries. For Aristotle, our practices of praise and blame, exhorting and discouraging, commanding and prohibiting, would make no sense if virtue could not be taught. The entire project of making laws and attaching rewards and punishments to laws would also be senseless if virtue could not be taught. Aristotle believed that *all* of the factors mentioned by Plato—teaching, practice, nature—were relevant to the imparting of virtue. In Aristotle's view, the reason we think that virtue is not teachable is that we make the mistake of identifying virtue with only what we have called 'intellectual virtue'.

Our approach to accounting ethics has so far been broadly Aristotelian in spirit. We follow Aristotle also in this regard. We maintain, with Aristotle, that accounting ethics can and should be promoted in all of the above ways, and that teaching is only one component in the imparting of virtue. In essence, the question, "Can ethics be taught?" is a complex question. Everything depends on what one means by 'ethics', and what one means by 'teaching'. When one draws the correct distinctions, then it becomes clear that ethics (in the appropriate sense) can indeed be taught (in the appropriate sense), and this result applies to accounting ethics as well.

Ten reasons why ethics (it seems) cannot be taught

Let us try to get clear about why people suspect that ethics cannot be taught. Here are ten reasons why.

(1) "If ethics can be taught, then it can be taught in a classroom. But no one could become ethical simply by taking classes." –If classroom instruction could impart ethics, then the effect would seem much greater than the supposed cause. How could something so mundane and ordinary as taking a class lead to something as distinctive as high ethical

behavior?   Also, the supposed effect seems different in kind from the supposed cause: being ethical is a matter of acting correctly; but being good at classwork is a matter of thinking, speaking, and writing correctly. No one could learn to be a good athlete, a good musician, or a good actor merely by sitting in a classroom. So how could someone learn to be a good human being in that way?

(2) "Being smart and being good are different.   Teaching can help someone become smart but not to be good."—Being smart, intelligent, clever, and being good, virtuous, ethical, are clearly two sorts of things. Some people are intelligent without being particularly good; other people are good without being particularly intelligent.   But only intelligence can be taught (partially so). So teaching has no effect on goodness. (And aren't there many examples of very clever accountants, who received excellent grades in courses in 'professional ethics' at the best business schools, who nonetheless went on in their professional life to commit egregious fraud?)

(3) "Our upbringing determines our character.   By the time anyone might attempt to teach us about ethics, it's too late to learn—our character is already fixed."—Whether someone is ethical or not depends on his character. But people acquire the character that they have when they are growing up. They become honest or not, trustworthy or not, truthful or not, depending upon how they associate with their childhood friends, and depending upon how vigilant their parents are in raising them and in insuring that they spend time with the right sorts of friends. By the time someone attends (say) high school, his or her character is largely fixed.

(4) "There really is freedom of action.   In the same circumstance, and given the same upbringing and background, one person will act well and another person will not. Thus, teaching cannot reliably produce ethical behavior." –To say that something can be taught is to say that teaching reliably produces it. For instance, piano playing can be taught, because taking piano lessons reliably produces skilled piano playing for the most part (not in every case, and not in the same degree, but nonetheless

there is a reliable connection). But teaching cannot reliably produce ethical action, because nothing reliably produces ethical action. Nothing does this, because our actions are essentially free. One can see this from how people react to a tragedy or disaster, say, the sinking of the Titanic: some men courageously allowed women and children to get into the boats first; others groped and clawed desperately for their lives, not giving any thought to others. In the end, our actions are inherently and essentially free. Thus, nothing determines them, and thus, in particular, teaching does not do so.

(5) "People often do what they know they should not do. But classes only teach us what we should do; they can't make us actually do this." – The difficult thing about ethics is usually not knowing what we should do, but rather doing what we know we should do. It's very common for people to realize clearly what they should do, but act otherwise. It's even more common, perhaps, for people to know what they should do 'deep down', but to act against this. Dishonest and unethical behavior is not caused, then, by ignorance about what we should do, but by a kind of turning away from, or obscuring, of what we in some sense already realize is the right thing—a 'dulling' or 'darkening' of conscience, as it were. So the solution to unethical behavior does not lie in teaching and, in that sense, ethics cannot be taught.

(6) "Whether we act well or not depends on likes, dislikes, preferences, and incentives, which don't have much to do with teaching." –In the end, we do what we most want to do, and we most want to do what we like, prefer, or are pleased in doing. One person is honest—because he would not have liked acting dishonestly. Another person is dishonest—because that's what appealed the most to him. Thus, our likes and dislikes, our preferences and the incentives attached to our actions, ultimately steer us to act in one way or another. Teaching does not change these things.

(7) "What is called 'teaching ethics' is giving explicit reasons for what we already implicitly accept and follow. Hence if we do not already have implicit reasons to act ethically, then teaching ethics cannot be of any

help."—As explained in chapter 3 above, to teach ethics is to teach a theory of ethics. But a theory of ethics, properly understood, is the explicit systemization of what we already in some sense accept, implicitly so. Thus, if someone is not already ethical, ethical theory will have nothing to work with. Thus, ethics can be taught only to someone who is ethical already.

(8) "At the deepest level, everyone is selfish. Each person aims at his own self interest. So the best we can do is to arrange rewards and punishments in such a way that a person's pursuit of his own self-interest is in aligment with the 'ethical' behavior that society expects. But there is no possibility of 'teaching' someone to be 'ethical' beyond this." —We regard ethical behavior as valuable only because of what others would think, or because of punishments we would receive if caught.

(9) "If virtue could be taught, there would be recognized teachers and experts of ethics." As we saw, this objection was first stated by Plato. The form this objection might typically take today would be the claim that there are no objective, universally shared values. "Whose standards should we use?", someone might say, "Which values should we adopt? In fact, there are a variety of equally plausible ways of looking at behavior—none of these is privileged over any others."

(10) "If virtue could be taught, virtuous people would succeed in conveying it to their children—but they don't."—This is another objection first offered by Plato, as we saw. We might apply the objection to make it an argument against the possibility of professional ethics: if high standards of ethical behavior in accounting could be taught, then it would in fact be successfully conveyed by founders of accounting firms (such as Arthur Andersen) to successive generations of employees, just as technical accounting skill gets transmitted within firms. And yet firms fail to transmit ethical standards: to whit, Andersen.

It all depends on what you mean by 'ethics' and 'teaching'

And yet, even given all of these apparent problems, it would be strange if ethics could not be taught.

This is so for various general reasons. For instance, we said that for someone to be good is for him to have the traits that enable him to carry out his distinctive task well. To be good is to be good at carrying out one's distinctive task. But in every other case of someone's having some distinctive task to carry out, it is possible to teach someone to be good at this: for instance, we can teach someone to be a good carpenter, a good physician, a good outfielder in baseball, or a good engineer. But then, by the same token, it should be possible to teach someone to be a good professional, such as an accountant. A good accountant, as we saw, is someone who carries out well the distinctive task of an accountant— which would mean fostering trust and truthfulness in financial reporting. That is, it would mean being an ethical accountant. (As we saw, it is misguided to draw a distinction between being a good professional and doing that professional work ethically.)

Again, if to be good at X is simply to do X well, and if doing X can be taught, then it would seem that doing X well can be taught. How could it be possible to teach some task, but not possible to teach doing that task well? Being ethical at some work or in some task is simply a way of doing it, and if the doing of it can be taught, then that particular way of doing it can be taught.

Again, what would be the point of laws, or recommendations, or commands, or rewards and punishments, if what we say had no effect on how others act? But if what we say does have an effect, then ethics can be taught—in the minimal sense, at least, that what we say makes it easier for others to be ethical. (The same holds for the example we set or fail to set.)

But the question of whether accounting ethics in particular can be taught hinges on what we mean by accounting ethics. As Plato pointed out similarly in the *Meno*, the question of whether virtue can be taught depends upon our answer to the question, 'What is virtue?':

> I am certain that if you were to ask any Athenian whether being virtuous was something inborn or acquired, he would laugh in your face, and say: "Stranger, you have far too good an opinion of

me, if you think that I can answer your question. For I literally do not know what virtue is, and much less whether it is acquired by teaching or not." And I myself, Meno, living as I do in this region of poverty, am as poor as the rest of the world; and I confess with shame that I know literally nothing about virtue; and when I do not know the "what" of anything, how can I know the "what sort"? How, if I knew nothing at all of Meno, could I tell if he was handsome, or the opposite of handsome; rich and noble, or the reverse of rich and noble? Do you think that I could?

We can schematically present our discussion in chapter 4 above by remarking that ethics in accounting involves basically four components:

> 1. *Understanding.* A familiarity with, and understanding of, the principles of accounting and the rules which are meant to express and safeguard these principles—in particular, an understanding of how the rules depend upon the principles.
>
> 2. *Idealism.* The aim or resolve, which consists in placing the ideals of the profession of accounting over one's own interests (which we identified, roughly, as 'integrity').

Moreover, the ability actually to carry out consistently this aim or resolve, which includes:

> 3. *Character*, that is, having the virtues, and
>
> 4. *Culture*, that is, a workplace in which it is easy to do what is ethical.

Thus, ethical accounting involves Understanding; Idealism; Character; and Culture. So the question of whether accounting ethics can be taught resolves into the question of whether any or all of these components can be 'taught' and, if so, how they can be 'taught'.

But it is clear that they can be taught. Understanding of the principles of accounting can be taught precisely through classwork and study of the right sort. As we saw in chapter 2, the right sort of understanding is acquired through seeing how accounting rules express and safeguard accounting principles, so that a practitioner comes to see rules as in the service of principles, not rules as trumping principles. And that sort of understanding, we have argued, is acquired best if a practitioner is led in turn to see how the principles of accounting are grounded in the nature and distinctive work of an accountant. Thus, classwork, and a study of the fundamentals of accounting ethics—in the manner presented this text—is capable of imparting the requisite understanding.

Idealism of some sort is present in nearly everyone, except for extreme sociopathic personalities. "Hypocrisy is the tribute that vice pays to virtue", as La Rochefoucauld correctly remarked—but this implies that even a hypocrite has some sort of latent idealism, because otherwise how could he possibly know what others take ethical behavior to be?

But what one needs to do, however, is to appeal to a practitioner's idealism, or 'sense of honor' or 'highmindedness', as one might call it, and this would be to 'teach' this component of ethics.   Idealism becomes livelier, the more we express our admiration for ideals and act upon them; it becomes diminished and weakened, the less we express our admiration for them and act upon them.   Accounting firms can express their admiration for idealism by reviving the corporate 'lore' that involves their exemplary founders—stories from the lives of exemplary practitioners, such as Arthur Andersen and George Oliver May.   And any practitioner can give examples from his or her own experience of how it turned out that 'honesty is the best policy'.   Indeed, a firm might solicit examples of these and publish them in a newsletter, or incorporate into company workshops discussion sessions in which practitioners exchanged stories that brought home this point. Idealism in ethics especially tends to be fostered by our natural desire to imitate: we see an example in another of some behavior that we admire very much, and then we keep this in mind as we act, aiming to imitate it in the manner that we can. That is why morality can be taught and encouraged through stories, anecdotes, lessons, and exemplary lives.   Generally the profession of accounting needs to recover its humanistic dimension—accountants cannot be narrow professionals, but rather should be liberally educated men and women with specific professional skill.

But this is not to deny that the profession should take steps to test the motivation of those who aspire to be accountants and positively exclude those whose motives appear doubtful.   One might think, for instance, that any instances of dishonesty and misrepresentation as displayed in student life (e.g. cheating, plagiarism) should disqualify permanently a student from a career in accounting, just as breaking the law excludes a student from a future profession in law.

Character, as we saw, is formed by and tested in small things and first things. This component of ethical accounting can be 'taught', then, by any efforts to insure that a practitioner's work in these respects is exemplary. For instance, in small things: there should be a complete intolerance of dishonesty, misrepresentation, or action under conflict of interest in a firm as regards what a practitioner does even outside of an engagement—in such 'small matters' as the use of expense accounts; claiming of tax exemptions and deductions; and practices of billing. An accountant in who he or she is, and not simply as a 'job', should represent probity in financial matters, just as a physician is generally an advocate for good health. The right approach to 'first things' would involve such things as: counting as an argument against a certain kind of accounting treatment that one could easily be tempted to abuse it in future instances; an initial conservativism in decisions, and the recommended attitude of skepticism, as regards a new engagement; a sharp and uncompromising attitude when encountering the first instance of fraud in management, no matter how small or apparently insignificant; and so on.

Culture in a firm is determined above all by the 'tone at the top'— the example set by management of moderation and integrity, but it is fostered of course by practices which draw attention to and reward action in which practitioners apparently sacrifice personal advantage for the sake of principle and probity.

And so, in the end, the answer to the question, "Can accounting ethics be taught?" is straightforward. There is no difficulty in principle in teaching it; in fact, the means for imparting ethics in accounting are all familiar. The real question is: Do we really want to teach it? And here one might be reminded of the famous prayer of St. Augustine: "Lord, give me chastity—but not just yet."

But why the difficulty?

As Aristotle remarks in his *Ethics*, in order to see clearly that a view is true, it is necessary not only to argue for it directly, but also to explain why the false positions seemed to be true. Why does it seem that ethics cannot be taught?

Some of the difficulties stated above came from a confusion between Understanding (a matter of 'intellectual virtue', as we called it) and Idealism and Character (which involve motivation). Some components of ethics can be taught in the classroom: that we learn these well is necessary to being ethical, but not sufficient. "If ethics can be taught"—went the first objection—"then it can be taught in a classroom." Obviously, anything teachable in a classroom setting would involve intellectual virtue only. Virtue of character, which involves motivation, is instead inculcated through example; friendly advice; exhortation; rules and laws; and rewards and punishments. It is a matter of 'practice', in Plato's sense.

Again, it was claimed that "Being smart and being good are different", and that the former but not the latter can be taught. – However, there are two senses of 'being smart'. In one sense, this means mere technical proficiency or cleverness—how to get effectively what you want. For instance, 'aggressive' yet non-transparent accounting is like that, or accounting that observes the 'rules' but only to get what is in the practitioner's or the client's interests (and does not serve the public interest). In another sense, 'being smart' means sagacity, good judgment, prudence, real insight and understanding—the sort of practical intelligence that we admire as being itself remarkable. This sort of 'being smart' is inseparable from being good.

The argument that "our upbringing determines our character" is to some extent true. Character is fairly settled by the time someone begins a professional career, or even by the time one begins professional studies. But, although settled, it can change—certainly it can become worse (think of the example of a young idealist practitioner being instructed for the first time in the practical work of the profession by a cynical and not entirely upright older associate). Moreover, because of the importance of little things and first things, the initial experiences of a new practitioner in a firm, and the expectations of the firm, are crucial in settling that practitioner's 'professional character'—his or her 'standards' as a professional.

"There is freedom of action." Yes, but not unpredictability, if someone has the relevant virtues. For instance, consider trustworthiness. A good person is trustworthy. If you are a mountaineer, you can really trust a good fellow climber, who is both technically skilled and loyal. The actions of such a person are not at all unpredictable. You could say *exactly* how such a person would act—and you would stake your life on it. (Being a partner in a firm is remarkably similar: one stakes one's life and reputation on the predictability of his or her fellow partners.) Or, again, consider integrity: true integrity is unswerving and exceptionless. It is impossible to have integrity most of the time—to waver, vacillate, to be open to bribery or monetary inducements, is *ipso facto* to lack integrity.

"People often do what they know they should not do. Classes can teach us what we should do; they can't make us actually carry that out." —But this is another objection based on a conflation of intellectual virtue with the whole of virtue. To know what a person should do (which, by the way, is in some cases a great achievement) is what intellectual virtue achieves; but actually to carry it out is the work of other sorts of virtue— and these are acquired through 'practice' in the broad sense, not through class instruction.

"Whether we act well or not depends on our likes or dislikes"—yes, but these are malleable. A person who hates getting up early but sets her alarm for 5:30 a.m. and gets out of bed nonetheless, whether tired or not, will (in most cases) eventually turn into a 'morning person' who loves being up at sunrise. When a person first begins athletic training, he hates to run or lift weights; but after months on a training regimen, he hates not running or lifting weights. That is why one might say that the task of imparting accounting ethics is to bring a practitioner to the state where he or she dislikes anything that has the appearance of dishonesty, lack of independence, lack of objectivity, or lack of integrity.

"To teach ethics is to give explicit reasons for implicit practices, so we cannot teach someone to be good who isn't implicitly good already." But most people act correctly in most of what they do. Even a malicious murderer will for much of his time be doing the right thing—paying bills, observing traffic laws, not attacking or harming others. It is fair to say that most of us in most of what we do are committed implicitly to the right principles.

"Everyone is self-interested at the deepest level". Yet not everyone would act dishonestly if he could do so without getting caught. People can and do sacrifice their self-interest for the sake of a higher ideal: that's clear from observation. So it is false that all of us must always be 'self-interested'—that is, if by 'self-interested' one means 'selfish.'

"If virtue could be taught, there would be recognized teachers and experts." But there are. Everyone is potentially a good 'teacher' of ethics, because everyone (or nearly everyone) can recognize bad behavior well enough in others. (The trick is to recognize it also in oneself.) Typically the wisdom embodied in the laws of a society is a 'teacher' of ethics. And then anyone whose life is in some respects at least held up as an example (Mother Teresa, Martin Luther King), or whose writings are truly edifying or challenging (Thomas a Kempis, Marcus Aurelius), is also a recognized teacher of ethics.

"If virtue could be taught, then the children of virtuous parents would be virtuous." But the objection presupposes that anyone who has virtue is able to teach it. It takes "virtue can be taught" to be equivalent to "every virtuous person can teach virtue" (and perhaps also "only virtuous persons can teach virtue"). But why should one accept these further claims?

Conclusion: an analogy

We should replace the question, "Can ethics be taught?" with "Can we take effective steps to make it so that practitioners are less disposed to act unethically?" And then clearly the answer is 'yes'.

It helps to consider an analogy: consider the campaign against drunk driving. When twenty years ago various groups such as Mothers Against Drunk Driving (MADD) initiated a campaign in the United States against drunk driving, it would have been ridiculous for someone to argue: "There's no point in attempting that. Ethics can't be taught. Nothing can be done to make people less disposed to drink and drive." Rather, everyone recognized what steps should be taken, if in fact we had the 'will' to get tough on drunk driving. Our society adopted a many-dimensional approach. Increase legal penalties. Be more vigorous in arrest and prosecution. Institute classes in Driver's Ed courses. Buy time on major networks for advertising. Create a culture that 'frowns' on driving while drinking. Invent the new cultural role of 'designated driver' (which has since become part of ordinary language). Make people aware that drinking affects above all one's ability to recognize the effects of drinking on one's own judgment. Hold up European cultures as a model for us, which were more ethical in these regards.

Similarly, a multi-faceted approach to reform of the accounting profession is possible, and necessary—from principles-based education, to changes in the culture of firms, and a more exacting prosecution in law.

But here too perhaps the most basic question is not whether the profession *can* be reformed, but whether we *want* to reform it enough, so that we actually do so. "Can ethics be taught, that is to say, promoted?" Yes, certainly. "Are we *concerned* enough with the profession, in order to preserve and promote its ethical foundation in all of our efforts and actions as practitioners?" But this is something up to us. We do our part in upholding the high ideals of the profession, by how we approach our own professional work and responsibilities. This book has shown the way to do so. Beginning here and now, we can make definite resolutions, and take concrete steps, to promote unswervingly and with high integrity, principles-based accounting, true professionalism, and an honorable pride.

Chapter 7 Review
Learning Objectives and Questions for Review

Learning Objectives:

After reading this chapter you should be able to:
• Characterize the classical context of the question.
• Explain why people think that ethics cannot be taught.
• Describe the four components of ethical accounting.
• Explain how each of these components can in fact be taught.
• Reply to the reasons people have for thinking that ethics cannot be taught.

Questions for Review

1. What did Socrates reproach his fellow citizens with?
    a. Waging war constantly against the Persians.
    b. Being more concerned about wealth than virtue.
    c. Lack of education.
    d. Caring too much about how they looked.
2. What dialogue of Plato opens with the posing of the question of whether virtue can be taught?
    a. The *Republic*.
    b. The *Symposium*.
    c. The *Meno*.
    d. The *Apology*.
3. Which of the following is not a reason why Plato suspected that virtue was not knowledge?
    a. Because prominent virtuous men often fail to teach virtue to their children.
    b. Because there are no recognized experts in virtue.
    c. Because often the children of virtuous men turn out not to be virtuous.
    d. Because ethics is not quantifiable.

4. That very intelligent doctors and lawyers collaborated with Hitler's schemes to exterminate Jewish people but some simple villagers risked their lives and families to help might be thought to show:

    a. That higher education can turn people into moral monsters.

    b. The potential depravity of all human beings.

    c. The supremacy of reason over faith.

    d. The absolute distinction between intelligence and goodness.

5. That in a disaster like the Titanic some people act heroically and others act despicably might be taken to show:

    a. Our actions are completely unpredictable.

    b. Our actions are free.

    c. Teaching cannot reliably impart good character.

    d. All of the above.

6. True or false?: "To teach someone to be a good accountant is to teach him or her to be an ethical accountant."

7. A course which teaches practitioners to view accounting rules as in the service of principles, and not as trumping principles, would impart which component of ethical accounting?

    a. Culture.

    b. Understanding.

    c. Idealism.

    d. Character.

8. Who said "Hypocrisy is the tribute that vice pays to virtue"?

    a. Chesterton

    b. Menken

    c. Samuel Johnson

    d. La Rochefoucauld

9. Idealism in ethics is fostered especially by:

    a. A competitive spirit

    b. Frequent self-deprecation

    c. A desire to imitate

    d. Haughtiness

10. Which of the following is not a 'first thing' which is crucially important as regards a practitioner's character?

    a. An attitude of initial skepticism in an engagement.

    b. Decisions as to how to spend bonuses.

   c. An uncompromising attitude when encountering initial evidence of fraud.

   d. Conservativism and erring on the safe side.

11. A sign that accounting ethics has successfully been imparted to a practitioner is when he or she:

   a. Can give the right answers on a test on ethics.

   b. Has memorized the Code of Professional Conduct and all relevant rules and rulings.

   c. Positively dislikes being unethical.

   d. Has ethical friends.

Suggested answers

1. b. Socrates emphasized the incommensurably greater value of the *bonum honestum* over instrumental goods and challenged his fellow citizens to seek these goods in the appropriate priority.

2. c. The *Meno* is devoted to the question of whether virtue can be taught and concludes, hypothetically, that if virtue is knowledge, then it can be taught.

3. d. Plato did not share a presumption that is common today, that only quantifiable assertions can truly be regarded as knowledge.

4. d. But the example fails to show this, because evil is in the long run contrary to true intelligence—for instance, Hitler pursued his maniacal plans even when they were contrary to his own self-interest and could not possibly succeed; and Hitler and many of his associates were essentially turned into madmen by their focus on evil ends.

5. d. However, the example does not show this. Generally people's characters are revealed by tests and trials. At the same time, some very extreme trials are such that the overstress human nature and little can be deduced from them about the characters of the people who respond in different ways.

6. True, because of the interweaving of technical skill and ethical commitment in any profession, as explained in chapter 3 above.

7. b. Part of the 'understanding' or intellectual virtue of an accountant is to view rules as in the service of principles.

8. d. This saying derives from the cynical French moralist from the court of Louis XIV.

9. c. That is why good examples, especially among leadership, are so important for ethics.

10. b. All of the others are examples pertaining to the practice of accounting, where an initial decision sets down a kind of precedent for later action.

11. c. As Aristotle remarked, what we like or dislike is a good sign of what we in practice regard as inherently good or bad.

Questions for Review

Chapter 2

1. Which of the following is the same as a necessary condition?
    a. A *sine qua non*
    b. A hypothetical circumstance
    c. A definition
    d. A *de facto* condition
2. Which of the following is the same as a sufficient condition?
    a. an effect
    b. a cause
    c. a requirement
    d. a definition
3. The AICPA Code of Ethics includes the following statement: "In general, a person's activities would be considered audit-sensitive if such activities are normally an element of or subject to significant internal accounting controls." Which of the following terms in the statement does not require 'good judgment' to be interpreted correctly?
    a. 'In general'
    b. 'audit-sensitive'
    c. 'normally'
    d. 'significant'
4. Which of the following statements implicitly appeals to what a 'reasonable person' would think or conclude?

a. "If you did that, it would have the appearance of lacking independence."

b. "I think that an action like that appears lacking in independence."

c. "Smith thought your action lacked independence."

d. "He was not thinking clearly when he accused you of lacking independence."

e. Both a. and d.

f. Both b. and c.

5. If someone follows the rules of his profession, then he or she is a true professional. True or false?

6. All intelligent rule-following implies due diligence. True or false?

7. Denise is auditing AJA Furniture and expresses her opinion that the company's financial statement presents the condition of the company well. Later various executives of AJA were found to have committed large-scale fraud. Denise excuses herself, claiming that she was ignorant. Which of the following might reasonably imply that her ignorance was at least in part culpable?

a. She treated a very slight fraud by just one executive as immaterial.

b. She took for granted the company's report of outstanding revenue when the furniture market was generally slumping.

c. She used all reasonable but not all available analytic procedures.

d. She presumed good faith on the part of the executives.

e. a. or c.

f. a. or b.

8. Which of the following is a satisfactory characterization of greed?

a. Wanting enough wealth to live a comfortable life filled with pleasures.

b. Being content to have a greater net worth than of any of one's classmates from business school.

c. Never being wealthy enough, no matter how much one has.

d. Always trying to get something for nothing.

e. All of the above.

f. c. and d. only

9. Complete the following sentence from Aristotle. "It seems pretty much the same thing, to be satisfied with rhetorical arguments from a mathematician, and to expect _____ from a rhetorician."
 a. rhetorical arguments
 b. demonstrations
 c. probable arguments
 d. necessary truths

10. Complete the following sentence from Aristotle. "_____ does not corrupt or overturn just any working supposition that we may have—for instance, whether or not a triangle is composed of two right angles—but rather those working suppositions that involve action."
 a. Greed
 b. The love of money
 c. What pleases or distresses us
 d. Bad influences on our action

11. The claims that defendants' expert witnesses in *Simon* made about accounting were:
 a. Outrageously false.
 b. Prejudicial and interested.
 c. Largely false.
 d. In general true.

Chapter 3

1. Complete the following analogy. Everyday speaking : grammar :: ordinary ethical action :
 a. the Ten Commandments
 b. Federal Law
 c. a theory of ethics
 d. wisdom

2. Consequentialism is the view that the rightness or wrongness of an action depends solely upon:
 a. The agent's intention in doing that action.
 b. The consequences of that action.
 c. The action's conformity with the moral law.

d. The consistency of the action.

3. Which of the following is a good equivalent of the Categorical Imperative?

    a. Act in such a way that everyone else could do the same.

    b. Above all, do no harm.

    c. Act so as to repay good with good and evil with evil.

    d. Do only categorically correct actions.

4. Which of the following is not a cardinal virtue?

    a. courage

    b. moderation

    c. honesty

    d. justice

5. True or false: Sharpness is a virtue.

6. True or false: To have courage means to have no fear.

7. Which of the following is a virtue of character as opposed to an intellectual virtue?

    a. good judgment

    b. knowledge of rules of conduct

    c. honesty

    d. insight

8. People form associations:

    a. To accomplish what they cannot do individually.

    b. Because they are 'joiners'.

    c. To maximize fulfillment in life.

    d. Because it is inevitable that we form associations.

9. Which of the following is not an example of a common good?

    a. peace, for a nation.

    b. victory, for an army.

    c. time off, for a worker.

    d. profitability, for a company.

10. Complete the following line from Aristotle, *Nicomachean Ethics*, 2.1: "Thus, in one word, states of character arise _____".

    a. by chance

    b. from custom

    c. out of like activities

    d. as a result of careful study

11. True or false. According to the court in *Feit v. Leasco*, the primary reason for the securities laws is the protection of the investor.

Chapter 4

1. Which of the following is a pair of commensurable goods?
    a. safety, earrings
    b. diamonds, music
    c. knowledge, justice
    d. televisions, earrings
2. The Latin name for a good that is incommensurably higher than an instrumental good is:
    a. *cui bono*
    b. *pro bono*
    c. *bonum honestum*
    d. *bonum augmentum*
3. The virtue which involves a practitioner's recognition of the demands of professionalism is:
    a. integrity
    b. high-mindedness
    c. honesty
    d. sense of duty
4. True or false. To claim that the profession of accounting is self-regulating is the claim that rules for members should be promulgated by the AICPA and not by any external or governmental authority.
5. An example of the extreme degree of professionalism required of accountants is:
    a. working for relatively low salaries
    b. safeguarding of outstanding business success
    c. prestigious title ("C.P.A")
    d. service to unknown persons
6. An accountant's 'distinctive' or 'characteristic work' is:
    a. securing the conditions of trust
    b. telling it how it is
    c. uncovering fraud
    d. adhering to GAAP

7. Which of the following is not a distinctive virtue of an accountant?
    a. Competence
    b. Due Care
    c. Sense of the Public Interest
    d. Humility
8. Which of the following is an internal factor that can compromise independence?
    a. bad digestion
    b. anxiety
    c. greed
    d. distractedness
9. Intellectual objectivity should be distinguished from_____.
    a. intellectual subjectivity
    b. verbal objectivity
    c. intellectual competence
    d. independence of the intellect
10. The distinctive virtues of an accountant are best acquired in:
    a. noteworthy accomplishments
    b. new circumstances
    c. small matters
    d. college courses
    e. all of the above
    f. a. and b. only
    g. b. and c. only
    h. c. and d. only
11. True or false. The 'worker product immunity' denied in *U.S. v. Arthur Young* would be inconsistent with the presumed independence of an auditor.

Chapter 5

1. The basic cause of Enron's collapse was:
    a. bad investments
    b. accounting improprieties
    c. a sour economy
    d. regulation of the energy market

2. The value of debts shifted off-balance sheet by Enron using SPEs was about:

    a. 1.2 billion dollars

    b. 500 million dollars

    c. 40 billion dollars

    d. 100 billion dollars

3. Enron's use of SPEs may be likened to what sort of confidence game?

    a. a shell game

    b. a pyramid scheme

    c. a Ponzi scheme

    d. a Nigerian letter

4. Which of the following did Enron's CEO Jeff Skilling not offer to McLean by way of assurances?

    a. Mark-to-market accounting implies restricted cash-flow at times.

    b. Fluctuations in the energy market imply larger profits for Enron.

    c. Enron can 'securitize' at will its long-term energy contracts.

    d. Enron's debt will transfer risk to independent buyers.

5. Complete the following line from the Sherron Watkins 'whistleblower letter': "To the layman on the street, it will look like we recognized funds flow of $800mm from merchant asset sales in 1999 by selling to a vehicle (Condor) that we capitalized with _____."

    a. a promise of Enron stock.

    b. fabricated M-to-M earnings.

    c. less than 3% equity from investors.

    d. unrecognized M-to-M earnings.

6. Which of the following was not a topic of the February 2001 Andersen conference call about its Enron engagement?

    a. whether Enron's off-balance sheet debt was material.

    b. whether Enron's SPEs lacked real economic substance.

    c. the fees Andersen could expect in the future from its Enron business.

    d. whether investors were being misled.

7. True or false. Sherron Watkins' 'whistleblower letter' went above and beyond what would be expected of a CPA acting as a professional.

8. True or false. That an entity cannot be regarded as independent if it fails to have 3% equity, implies that it is independent if it does have 3% equity.

9. That Andersen signed off on Enron SPEs that in fact had less than 3% outside equity is an illustration of the principle that:

    a. Less is more.

    b. Always the more conservative course of action is best.

    c. Someone oblivious to the principle will not reliably follow the rule.

    d. Independence is guaranteed only by scrupulous attention to appearances.

10. It is speculated above that the first bad step of Andersen's Enron auditors was signing off on:

    a. extensive use of mark-to-market accounting

    b. an SPE for Enron's office building

    c. excessive executive compensation

    d. obscure footnotes in Enron's yearly report

Chapter 6

1. What event made possible the founding of the company that was later to become WorldCom?

    a. a man walks on the moon

    b. the transcontinental railway

    c. the breakup of AT&T

    d. the fall of the Soviet Empire

2. Who was the internal auditor who presented evidence of WorldCom fraud to the Audit Committee in April 2002?

    a. Sherron Watkins

    b. Kim Emigh

    c. Cythia Cooper

    d. Tony Minert

3. What E/R number was the industry analysts' target for WorldCom?

    a. 24%

    b. 50%

    c. 12%

   d. 42%

4. Approximately how much of accrual funds was improperly released in 1999-2000?

   a. 60 billion

   b. 3.3. billion

   c. 1 billion

   d. 800 million

5. A judgment that happens to coincide with one's own self-interest is an _____ judgment.

   a. interested

   b. interesting

   c. arresting

   d. impartial

6. What euphemism did WorldCom internal accountants use for capitalized line costs?

   a. accounting 'fluff'

   b. non-cash adjustments

   c. mystery acquisitions

   d. Scott Sullivan's goody bag

7. What was the small step of cooperation with the Nazis that Dutch physicians refused to take?

   a. saluting Hitler with "Sieg Heil!"

   b. wearing the Swastika

   c. rehabilitating of the sick for useful labor

   d. giving physicals to SS officers

8. How did Andersen describe its relationship to WorldCom?

   a. 'detached observer'

   b. 'societal watchdog'

   c. 'long-term partner'

   d. 'conscience'

9. True or false: Andersen said it would reject the traditional audit approach in auditing WorldCom?

10. True or false: In the course of its audits, Andersen consulted the General Ledger of WorldCom.

Chapter 7

1. What reward did Socrates receive for devoting his life to exhorting his fellow citizens to care about being virtuous?

    a. the death penalty

    b. absolute political power

    c. exile

    d. publicly provided meals for life

2. What was Plato's verdict on the question of whether virtue can be taught?

    a. Virtue cannot be taught.

    b. Virtue can be taught if virtue is a kind of knowledge.

    c. Virtue can be taught only by philosophers.

    d. Virtue is taught by imitation.

3. Which of the following is not a reason given above for why it seems that classroom learning could not impart virtue?

    a. You can't teach someone to be a good athlete by classroom learning, and similarly you can't teach someone to be virtuous in that way.

    b. Classroom learning by its nature produces conformity, but ethics implies individuality.

    c. Classroom learning can at best change how we think, but thoughts are powerless to oppose strong impulses.

    d. Classroom learning helps us to think or speak better, but ethics involves acting better.

4. Which of the following is consistent with the view that ethics can be taught?

    a. We act ethically only when it is in our interest to do so.

    b. Power corrupts, and absolute power corrupts absolutely.

    c. All human beings are inherently selfish.

    d. No one does an ethical action simply because it is intrinsically good.

5. That the ethical ideals of Arthur Andersen were not preserved or transmitted to successive generations of accountants within the firm that he founded, whereas technical accounting skill was, might be taken to show:

    a. All standards are relative.

b. Ethical ideals are not knowledge.

c. Andersen was ineffective as a founder.

d. Technical skill grows at a faster rate than ethical knowledge.

6. In order to answer the question, "Can ethics be taught?", we must first answer the question of:

a. What ethics is.

b. What the meaning of 'is' is.

c. Whether ethics and teaching are distinct.

d. What the meaning of life is.

7. Which of the following is not a basic component of ethical accounting?

a. culture.

b. character.

c. savvy.

d. idealism.

8. Which of the following is not a way in which the accounting profession can foster idealism in accounting?

a. Recover the humanistic dimension of accounting.

b. Screen more carefully aspirants to the profession for good character.

c. Retell anecdotes of accounting which illustrate that 'honesty is the best policy'.

d. Offer courses on idealism in accounting.

9. The phrase 'tone at the top' indicates which component of ethical accounting?

a. Understanding

b. Idealism

c. Character

d. Culture

10. Which of the following is not a 'small thing' in which probity and scrupulous honesty should be expected in an accountant?

a. Use of expense accounts.

b. Claims for tax deductions.

c. Billing practices.

d. Drafting of the engagement letter.

About the Authors

MARK CHEFFERS (mcheffers@ivesinc.com) is the Founder and CEO of IVES Group, Inc., an independent research provider focused on advancing risk assessments and market intelligence in the areas of public company non-financial indicators, public company auditing and accounting malpractice. IVES' primary programs include: www.AccountingMalpractice.com, www.AuditAnalytics.com, www. SECanalytics.com and www.LegalCaseDocs.com. IVES counts as its clients some of the largest professional service, research, regulatory and insurance organizations in the world. Mr. Cheffers is additionally a researcher, author, accounting ethics advisor and litigation consulting specialist. Prior to founding IVES Group, Mr. Cheffers was a Manager at PricewaterhouseCoopers, before operating a successful litigation consulting firm, specializing in financial investigations and litigation consulting for large and complex professional malpractice assignments. Mr. Cheffers has been integrally involved in the start-up of several ventures, including one of the largest Charter Schools in the United States. He is a member of the American Institute of Certified Public Accountants (AICPA) and has achieved their Accredited Business Valuation (ABV) professional designation. Mr. Cheffers has a BSBA, magna cum laude, in accounting and finance from Boston University, and an MBA from the Harvard Business School. Mr. Cheffers is a regular commentator in the major financial press on matters of accounting malpractice and corporate governance, as well as a sought-after speaker on these issues.

MICHAEL PAKALUK (mpakaluk@clarku.edu) received his A.B. from Harvard College, M. Litt. from the University of Edinburgh, and Ph.D. in philosophy from Harvard University, where he studied ethics and political philosophy under John Rawls, who also supervised his dissertation. He is Associate Professor of Philosophy at Clark University and has held visiting positions at Brown University, St. Andrews University, and Cambridge University. The author of *Other Selves: Philosophers on Friendship* (Hackett, 1991), *Aristotle's Nicomachean Ethics VIII and IX: Translation with Commentary* (Oxford, 1998), and *Aristotle's Nicomachean Ethics: An Introduction* (Cambridge, 2005), he has also published widely in scholarly and popular journals. Dr. Pakaluk is recognized as one of the world's leading experts in classical ethics. He has served as Trustee of the Worcester Public Library; Founder and Trustee of the Abby Kelley Foster Regional Charter School in Worcester; and Founder and Trustee of the American Public Philosophy Institute. He is currently Director of the Boston Area Colloquium in Ancient Philosophy. Dr. Pakaluk resides in Lancaster, Massachusetts, with his wife and children.

Index